Toward Improving Canada

Dave Amonson

First edition published 2015

10 9 8 7 6 5 4 3 2 1

Amonson, Dave

Toward Improving Canada / Dave Amonson

ISBN-13: 978-0-9940597-4-1 Printed book

ISBN-13: 978-0-9940597-5-8 eBook

Dedication

To those who prefer rational government built on the expectation of individual responsibility with room for deserved compassion.

Preface

Howdy, Neighbour. You're embarking on a voyage of discovery. Many will relish the trip and will return with good feelings and resolutions to make many similar excursions. Many will step on board with heavy heart believing they are leaving a comfortable, compassionate, reliable home for a new destination foreign to their experience and pre-ordained to provide a life of misery and woe. For the fearful folks, I hope to provide reassurance and understanding so the new home becomes a pleasant surprise. When you analyze the thrust of my proposals, you'll see rationality bubbles to the surface wherever you let it. While you may be fearful and uncertain, friendly neighbours will provide support, but they'll expect you to adapt to the new surroundings and do your part to be independent, good neighbours too.

Many focus on what's wrong with Canada. I wish to be more upbeat and constructive. My proposals do not dwell on the absurdities we can find with little effort; rather, I hope my proposals will be likened to a new commercial product built, packaged, merchandised, and consumed by the masses. The merchandising strategy should emphasize the good points, work at eliminating the weak points, pay ongoing attention to quality, continue searching for better answers, take cognizance of the views of critics, and generally strive for the acceptance of those solid citizens who are ignored by bleating pockets of society.

My parents operated a small, mixed farm where they, along with their neighbours, homesteaded a new district. Dad arrived with nothing but a grade twelve education and confidence in himself. He was 19 years old. Mom came with her family to the district and had, as her dowry, a small packet of wheat seed. In 1929, these were meagre beginnings. From those few resources, my parents raised five children, developed a productive farm, coached baseball, acted as executives on church, civic, and farm boards, built roads, bridges, houses, and imposed no burden on government. While my parents are special in my eyes, the whole community was populated with people who took individual responsibility and built a thriving community out of virgin land.

While the environment changes over time, individual responsibility is inherent in most of us. It can blossom again if our systems expect it.

During my high school years, I raised sheep. I bought six ewes and a ram from a neighbour. From that nucleus, and more acquisitions, I built a flock and gained valuable experience. While the sheep raising initiative was not earthshaking, two incidents affected my development.

I arranged to sell four lambs through the livestock cooperative. It was customary for the co-op to give a cash advance on the livestock. I got a cash advance on my lambs and waited for the final payment to arrive. When it came, I eagerly opened the envelope and read the cheque. My heart stopped. The cheque showed all zeroes. My cash advance had been more than the net value of the lambs sold. An accompanying letter asked for something like $4.21 back from me. Many people believe business is all pleasure and no pain. They should try being a fifteen year-old running a sheep empire!

One day in the heat of summer, I noticed a ewe standing apart from the flock and looking peaked. I went over to her and she did not walk away as most animals would in an open setting. I decided to move her back to the barn where I could provide some medicine. I grabbed the wool on her back to steer her toward the barn and the wool came away from her back. Beneath her wool was a crawling mass of maggots. It nearly turned my

Preface

stomach as I removed all the loose wool and ushered the ewe to a corral. The only medicine I could find was peroxide. I poured it on the maggots. It fizzed. The ewe returned to health. Each following year, after I sheared the flock, I could identify the maggot infested ewe by the different colour on her back and reflect on the vivid incident.

I look back on the maggot incident and see a metaphor for the present Canadian situation. On the surface, Canada looks a little ragged, but many assume the underlying structure is sound.

However, there are lots of places in the Canadian system where maggots are flourishing. I invite you to tug on the wool around you and, if maggots are found, persevere in a cure. You will find an appropriate medicine. Let's at least decide some medicine would be helpful.

I'm sometimes teased about being "Little David, the shepherd boy." I take the teasing well because: I believe the sheep initiative helped me on the road to believing in individual responsibility and independent enterprise; I like to tease, so I have learned to take teasing in stride; and I like to swim against the current, much as the biblical David took on an apparently overpowering Goliath. I hope my contribution to the debate about Canada's future will be disproportionately positive.

We grew up with teeter-totters. The simple structures provided hours of recreation for children. We discovered modest adjustments in the distance from the pivot point would adjust the balance to close to equilibrium. Let's change the name of the teeter-totter to taker-maker. Let's assume there is a physical stop at the far ends of the taker-maker. These physical stops are comprised of the truly needy on the taker end, and the cream of productive society on the maker end. We recognize there is a small percentage of truly needy which we are prepared to support. This small percentage does not change much over time. On the other end, there are a few individuals who thrive no matter how many hurdles and inequities we hurl in their path. Inhibiting these folks is a tragedy which not only affects them but many around who would benefit from their initiatives.

In between the two extremes is a multitude; let's say 95% of the population. I hypothesize this group, like a puddle of mercury, is nestled up against the taker end of the taker-maker. We have allowed our systems to make the taker end heavier than the maker end. We will disagree on how unbalanced the taker-maker is today, but my observation is the taker end has gained substantial weight over the last half century. This includes whole generations who have experienced welfare as their way of life (whether or not this can be said to be their own fault). It also includes baby boomers who started out on a kinder, gentler path and created an inept system that will fail as they add more weight to the taker end. How do we add weight to the maker end? I believe the answer lies in improving individual responsibility and reducing collective abuse of power.

This is the theme of this book. Welcome to a rational Canada with room for deserved compassion.

"Man cannot survive except through his mind. He comes on earth unarmed. His brain is his only weapon. Animals obtain food by force. Man has no claws, no fangs, no horns, no great strength of muscle. He must plant his food or hunt it. To plant, he needs a process of thought. To hunt, he needs weapons, and to make weapons -- a process of thought. From this simplest necessity to the highest religious abstraction, from the wheel to the skyscraper, everything we are and everything we have comes from a single attribute of man -- the function of his reasoning mind.

But the mind is an attribute of the individual. There is no such thing as a collective brain. There is no such thing as a collective thought. An agreement reached by a group of men is only a compromise or an average drawn upon many individual thoughts. It is a secondary consequence. The primary act -- the process of reason -- must be performed by each man alone. We can divide a meal among many men. We cannot digest it in a

Preface

collective stomach. No man can use his lungs to breathe for another man. No man can use his brain to think for another. All the functions of body and spirit are private. They cannot be shared or transferred." C. S. Peirce (1839-1914); Collected Papers, Ayn Rand; The Fountainhead.

Chapter 1 Life Security

Canadians take a global view of our safety net. They gloss over the individual in need and assume some broad government program will work. This assumption is wrong. We need to focus on a specific individual and develop a plan with the individual. In business jargon, we need to "empower" the individual. This cannot be done at any government level. It has to be done at the individual level. My proposals facilitate the empowerment of a majority of individuals who would otherwise rely on government support.

The keys to the proposal are: recognize human nature exists; harness human nature for positive rather than negative reinforcement; make the assumption a majority in any society are naturally responsible, given a chance; make the assumption a majority of folks are more rational than many opinion influencers will acknowledge; and be sure the alternatives to individual responsibility are significantly below the levels capable folks will choose to follow. Once we have dealt with the masses, we are all willing, and able, to provide for the truly needy.

"Good sense is the best distributed thing in the world: for everyone thinks himself so well endowed with it that even those who are the hardest to please in everything else do not usually desire more of it than they possess. In this it is unlikely that everyone is mistaken. It indicates rather that the power of judging well and of distinguishing the true from the false -- which is what we properly call 'good sense' or 'reason' -- is naturally equal in all men." René Descartes (1596-1650); Discourse,

Philosophical Writings of Descartes, trans. J. Cottingham, R. Stoothoff and D. Murdoch, I. p. 111

How do we get there from here? The Life Security Plan harnesses the human nature of the masses. There are four general categories for which the Life Security Plan will not suffice:

1. The physically and mentally handicapped who cannot function independently,

2. The relatively unfortunate who were once able to meet the Life Security Plan requirements, but who have suffered setbacks which drained all of their resources, including their Life Security Plan funds,

3. The economic underperformers who have not yet achieved the median funding required by the Life Security Plan, and

4. Those who choose to default on individual responsibility.

Individuals in the first two categories will see the government support them at a standard acceptable to the majority of the ordinary folks in control at the time of need.

Individuals in the third category will struggle along without formal assistance or undergo more screening with the expectation they will accept a non-government program to become financially independent, or they will choose to land in the fourth category.

Individuals in the fourth category make a lifestyle decision. Government support will be the barest of minima (i.e. subsistence). The individuals who stay in this category very long cannot be saved with any amount of money (because money is not the problem).

What is involved in the Life Security Plan? Life is sprinkled with funding situations. Most of these needs, in the first seventy years of each individual's life, are periodic, unpredictable, and sometimes dramatic. In retirement years, the needs become more routine, but still haphazard. The prevalent mood in Canada has been government must provide support for these life security needs. The trouble is human nature gets in the way. Whenever something is free or inexpensive, the demand goes up disproportionately. Many people adopt the attitude "everybody else does it, why can't I?" The Life Security Plan changes this mentality. It says to ordinary folks: you already know, and accept, you are primarily responsible for home, food, clothing, and child care; you are also primarily responsible for life security. Yes, there will be a fallback position, but your primary protection is your own commitment; and the government will provide "normal" care to those who have diligently followed the Life Security Plan guidelines, but your financial independence will be dramatically reduced before the government support kicks in.

Many folks will ask, "How can I afford the costs of a Life Security Plan?" The answer is twofold: you need a feasible plan; and, if middle income folks are the bulk of the population and they can't afford it, who is going to pay for it? Rationality might play a part.

You will be familiar with the Consumer Price Index; an indicator of inflation reflected by the cost of a basket of goods and services bought by Canadians. The Life Security Plan will be modelled on a similar index, called the Security Plan Index, which will reflect the median cost of the basket of life security items for each year of age of an individual. From the Security Plan Index, actuaries will build a Life Security Plan curve reflecting the target amount of funds each individual should have in his or her Life Security Plan for their present age from birth to, say, age 110. The actual amounts of life security costs from birth throughout puberty are very low. Individuals run into pregnancy, dental care, traffic accidents, job losses, and serious illness. Actuaries will develop a typical curve taking into account these various episodes while allowing the individual's Life Security Plan to grow to an amount sufficient to provide retirement income, nursing home care, acute care, and hospice. The Life Security Plan curve will reflect the median costs of these eventualities. It will not cover the highest costs that might be incurred by any particular individual. The governments' general funds will cover the extreme costs once the Life Security Plan and the individual's other resources have been exhausted.

How might a family with modest income fund the Life Security Plans for each member of the family? This is dealt with in the Individual Obligations chapter, but the principal is this:

A household unit contains, say, a family of four;

The annual income of the household is established, say, $58,000;

Each individual files a tax return on his or her birthday;

Mom's Life Security Plan expects her to have $147,000 in her plan. She presently has $143,400, so she needs $3,600 to top up her plan to target;

Dad's Life Security Plan expects him to have $175,000 in his Life Security Plan. He presently has $172,000, so he needs $3,000 to top up to target;

Daughter's Life Security Plan expects her to have $12,000 in her plan. She presently has $11,000, so she needs $1,000 to top up her plan; and

Son's Life Security Plan expects him to have $6,000 in his plan. He presently has $6,000, so he doesn't need to top up his plan.

Each individual files his or her Individual Obligations return on his or her birth date anniversaries with the following impacts:

Life Security

Description	Mom	Dad	Daughter	Son	Total
Household income	34,000	24,000			58,000
Number of household members	1	1	1	1	4
Average income per individual in household	14,500	14,500	14,500	14,500	
Personal exemption	(5,000)	(5,000)	(5,000)	(5,000)	
	9,500	9,500	9,500	9,500	
Individual obligation @ 50%	4,750	4,750	4,750	4,750	19,000
Life Security Plan requirement	(3,600)	(3,000)	(1,000)	-	(7,600)
Taxes to be paid in total (to all tax levels)	1,150	1,750	3,750	4,750	11,400

The effective household tax rate, for all governments in this example, is 20% ($11,400/$58,000).

Points to notice in the above example are: every individual gets the same personal exemption regardless of age, creed, gender, marital status, or any other trait; the individual obligation is the same for every individual in the household (the household is defined by the occupants; not any bureaucracy); any tax otherwise owing is reduced by the amount of funds required to bring the Life Security Plan of the individual up to the published target curve; any excess (up to the maximum) after the Life Security Plan has been topped up is sent to the governments as general tax revenues. The effective household tax rate is not static. It could be zero if the Life Security Plan requirements absorbed all of the individual obligations.

One of the rhetorical tools of opponents of individual responsibility is the retort "not on the backs of the poor!" The Life Security Plan and Individual Obligations plans are designed to recognize the need to be rational by allowing the poor to first take care of day-to-day needs, then life security needs; and only then contribute to general government funding. Those who do not meet the Life Security Plan curve expectations will be more vulnerable to the future majority decisions as to "normal" care when their Life Security Plan and other resources are exhausted

11

and they request help from the government. Individual responsibility and peer pressure will yield positive results under the Life Security Plan concept; all health and dental facilities will be privately-owned and operated. Competition will set the fair value of these services. Government and private health plans cause our medical and dental services to be distorted by lack of individual responsibility. Whenever the government is called upon to provide individuals with these services, the market price will already be well-known. There will be talk of a two-tier system. I respond, "There is already a 30,000,000-tier system in Canada, and tears should be shed for the waste in the present so-called universal systems".

Health protection is a defining trait of Canadians. To the extent we find a feasible model, Canadians will continue to endorse universal health protection. The challenge is to design the health protection model so it benefits from human nature rather than suffers from it. The Life Security Plan is a comprehensive safety net built on the strengths of human nature. If you cannot find rationality in the Life Security Plan, the ideas in this book will be incompatible with your views.

You might wonder how the present systems could integrate into the Life Security Plan model. Here are a few ideas: present registered retirement savings plans, registered retirement investment funds, pension plans, and the like could be transferred into the Life Security Plan model with little fanfare; and the present value of quasi-contractual existing programs such as Old Age Security, Canada Pension Plan, employment insurance, and workers' compensation could be transferred into the Life Security Plan's as Special Canada Bonds (workers' compensation would result in Special Provincial Bonds) which will be used last by the Life Security Plan owner and, if not used, will lapse at death.

Those who fare well throughout their lifetimes, or who die without using their retirement amounts or incurring major costs,

Life Security

will have funds left in their Life Security Plan's. These funds are personal assets which are totally untaxed.

While the definition of income will be left to the accounting profession, the beneficiaries will have "income" equal to their share of proceeds from a Life Security Plan whether it be their own Life Security Plan or inherited.

Any "special bonds" issued as part of the transition to the new program will lapse on death and not be available for inheritance.

No individual will be allowed to borrow from any Life Security Plan nor direct the investments of individual Life Security Plans. These lending and investment functions will be done by financial institutions independent of the holders of individual Life Security Plans.

Under no circumstances will the Life Security Plan be subject to third party claims. A specific pledge, divorce, bankruptcy, or personal guarantee will not extend to the amounts in a Life Security Plan. The financial community shall guarantee the funds, including interest, in the Life Security Plans. The only way to get at the Life Security Plan of an individual is for the individual to initiate withdrawals for life security expenditures.

Mandatory Savings

"For all men are by nature provided of notable multiplying glasses, that is, their passions and self-love, through which, every little payment appeareth a great grievance; but are destitute of those prospective glasses, namely moral and civil science, to see far off the miseries that hang over them, and cannot without such payments be avoided." Thomas Hobbes (1588-1679); Leviathan, English Works, 3, p. 170

An unrepentant libertarian would reject any move to force an individual to save for future events. Starting with the premise a majority of Canadians are not willing to let people die in the streets, this model consciously chooses to compromise the basic libertarian ideal to find a model that will provide some broad discipline, while preserving as much individual responsibility as deemed rational.

The Life Security Plan observes: too many individuals will live for today and not provide for the reasonable expected obligations of tomorrow, when individuals fail to provide for tomorrow, and tomorrow arrives, the rest of Canadians feel obligated to step into the breach, therefore, Canadians have concluded they should impose some level of mandatory savings on every individual consistent with the individual's ability to save.

Such mandatory savings shall be structured to preserve as much individual responsibility as deemed rational. This means the savings shall not be removed from the individual's control, but shall provide a reliable accumulation vehicle and an efficient "sober second thought" withdrawal model. While the money saved is the individual's money, the model is structured so self-interest dictates most individuals will choose to save rather than remit additional taxes. The key is to get human nature working for positive reinforcement.

The model ensures individual responsibilities are preserved. The basic hierarchy is: food, clothing, shelter, child care, utilities, transportation; life security; basic national government; municipal government; provincial government; and, federal non-basic programs.

Life Security Plan

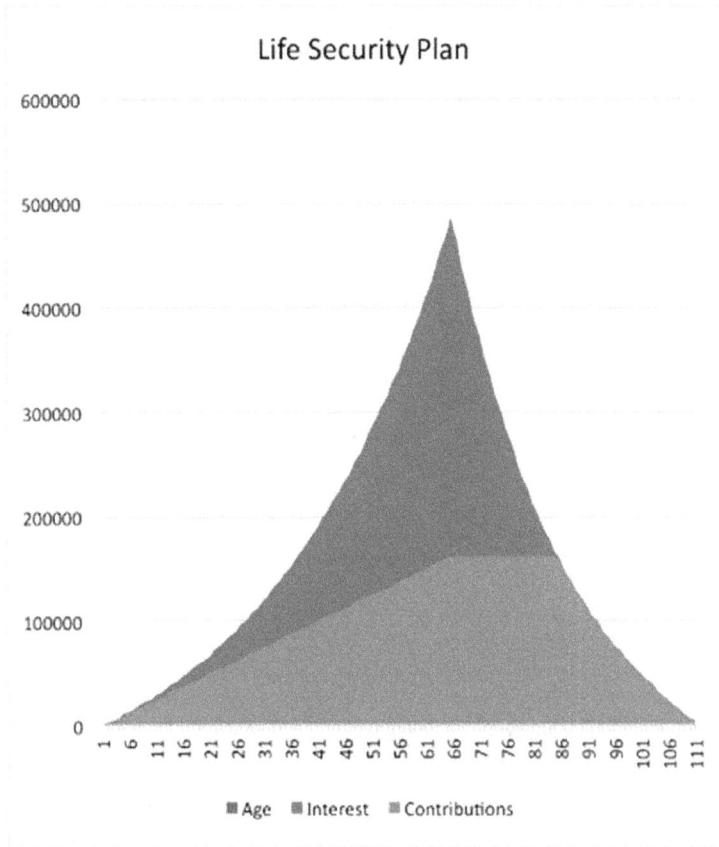

■ Age ■ Interest ■ Contributions

The vertical axis shows the amount in the Life Security Plan for each year of a median life.

The horizontal axis shows the age of a median individual up to age 111.

The assumptions include: annual contributions of $2,500 to age 65, interest of 3% on remaining balance, retirement withdrawals of $38,000 per annum commencing at age 66 with declining amounts as fewer individuals live to age 111.

Chapter 2 Controlling Spending

My philosophy leans toward individual responsibility and independent enterprise and little state interference. I do not intend to impose my bias on the masses. I point out how the majority can direct the state's involvement. There is ample room for all philosophies and political views to be expressed and merchandised. But there is less room for special interest groups to impose government intervention on the reluctant majority.

The British democratic model has much to recommend it. I propose leaving most of the model in place. Representative democracy breaks down when elected representatives venture beyond intended territory. Their authorized territory should be a point of debate. Some believe this is for the electorate to decide, but periodic elections do not chunk the policies of each major Party to allow voters to provide effective guidance once the ruling Party is decided. There is still room for elected representatives; they just need tighter guidance. For purposes of this book, I've circumscribed their territory with three strands on the fence. Each strand has a binding purpose.

Strand 1: Each level of government shall not spend more than it receives. Tax revenues are trust funds which shall not to be overspent.

Strand 2: The majority who fund programs shall have the say on which programs will be maintained.

Strand 3: No individual shall be forced to pay more tax than the majority of individuals in the jurisdiction pay.

Strand 1 stipulates no government ever budgets to run a deficit. The standard rebuttal is deficits are good in a recession economy. Who is gullible enough to believe governments are smarter in a downturn than they are in any other segment of the business cycle? Once a deficit of any amount is tolerated, Strand 1 is not just stretched, it's broken. We must not let our fence fall into disrepair. It needs all three strands.

Strand 2 requires majority approval (by those who pay) on a program-by-program basis. This begs the questions: how do you get majority feedback on a program-by-program basis and how do you know the majority understands what each program accomplishes? These questions are answered in the next chapter.

Strand 3: ensures no individual shall pay more tax than the majority of individuals in the jurisdiction pay.

Every resident indicates the government spending programs the resident both supports in principle and is able, and willing, to pay for in fact. This does not eliminate the role of the elected representatives, but it does put a "fence" around the groups of programs governments can sustain.

You will find areas in the proposal you think will require refinement. Many concerns have already been addressed, but I recognize there will be more.

As you study this chapter, consider how well the plan responds to our many complaints about the existing system:

The system doesn't work!

We don't have a say!

Get the government out of the economy!

Lobby groups have too much influence!

Government expenditures occur with little public support!

The quiet majority has no mechanism to effect change!

The individual can't do anything!

We have four-year dictatorships in Canada!

There are too many hidden taxes!

There are too many hidden expenditures!

Controlling Spending

"A crowd . . . in its very concept is the untruth, by reason of the fact that it renders the individual completely impenitent and irresponsible, or at least weakens his sense of responsibility by reducing it to a fraction." Soren Kierkegaard (1813-1855); The Point of View for my Work as an Author, trans. W. Lowrie, p. 112

We see the decisions of a collective few overpowering the wishes of many individuals. The plan corrects most of the flaws in the present system. It obligates every resident to complete an annual return on or before his or her birthdate, and shifts the power to the wishes of the paying majority on a line-by-line basis. This is an improvement over periodic referenda because it is cost efficient, makes the task of lobby groups formidable, and it's automatic. It puts major chunks of decision-making into the hands of the quiet majority, who will, for the first time, have a strong, effective voice.

The substance of the proposal can be summarized in the following statements: all levels of government must be precluded from budgeting peace-time deficits; all levels of government shall be required to retire all existing debt within 25 years; all residents must be allowed to indicate their majority approval or disapproval of generic groups of government spending programs on their annual returns, and such majority indications shall be binding on the governments; and all mandatory government programs shall be wholly funded from personal taxes.

Most rhetoric directed at government inadequacies contains no viable alternative to the existing system. For example, tax and expenditure limitations are too cumbersome, confrontational, and ad hoc to achieve the steady control required. This plan is a viable alternative.

Canada has evolved as a peace-loving, compassionate, generous, cooperative country. This reputation appeals to the majority. The mindset tends to erode self-reliance and individual responsibility. This cannot be democratically controlled unless a majority of the population is willing, and able, to pay an equal price for government programs.

Toward Improving Canada

The spending plan controls government while preserving a role for elected representatives and Senators. It imposes a workable fence around the field within which governments must operate.

The essential ingredients of the fence are: democratically elected representatives can establish policy, provide leadership, provide a forum for useful debate and provide education about issues, but they must include a stewardship function; the government must not spend what it does not have; there shall be no peacetime deficit; government sources of revenue shall be limited to a combination of voluntary participation in programs and revenues generated by the plan.

The above essential ingredients can form a workable tax structure. Government revenue for a given year will be established as follows: estimated program revenues (from voluntary programs); plus estimated corporate tax; plus estimated non-resident tax; plus estimated personal tax revenues. Municipal and provincial governments will not have access to any portion of corporate nor non-resident taxes. Tax revenue will be sufficient to cover the estimated costs of all active programs. It will be sufficient to amortize the historical cumulative deficit over 25 years with blended principal and interest payments, plus the last year's actual deficit, plus a cushion equal to last year's deficit.

Every individual is equal under the law. Therefore, every resident should pay an equal tax under the law. This is recognized to be impossible since a portion of the residents cannot, because of circumstances, pay anything, let alone an equal amount. There is a base point which is accepted as a democratic principle, "majority rules". Under this concept, if a majority are not willing, and able, to pay an equal amount for a program, then the majority rules the program will not continue.

Where governments provide services to the less fortunate, it is out of a sense of compassion and fair play, not out of an inherent right of the less fortunate.

Controlling Spending

A spending system should have the following objectives: to provide a stable, predictable environment for the population; to foster individual responsibility and initiative; to recognize all citizens are equal before the law and democracy will only work where the net costs of programs are supported, equally, by more than fifty percent of the residents; and to minimize the structure required to achieve appropriate government funding.

Individual Obligations

Every resident will submit an annual return on or before the anniversary of his or her birthdate. The annual return will be limited to the digital equivalent of one side of four 8.5" x 11" pages: the first page will be the Individual Obligations Form; the second page will be the Municipal Approval Form; the third page will be the Provincial Approval Form; and the fourth page will be the Federal Approval Form.

In addition to showing the amount of personal tax actually being remitted, each individual shall show approval or disapproval of each and every generic program category on the three approval forms. Approvals of programs shall not be honoured if the cumulative budgeted equal costs of the approved programs exceed the amount remitted. This precludes any individual from indicating approval of programs for which the full equal budgeted cost of the approved programs is not remitted by that individual.

"I know of no safe depository of the ultimate powers of the society but the people themselves; and if we think them not enlightened enough to exercise their control with a wholesome discretion, the remedy is not to take it from them, but to inform their discretion." Thomas Jefferson; from Against the Current Trudeau, p. 76

"Good sense is the best distributed thing in the world: for everyone thinks himself so well endowed with it that even those who are the hardest to please in everything else do not usually

desire more of it than they possess. In this it is unlikely that everyone is mistaken. It indicates rather that the power of judging well and of distinguishing the true from the false -- which is what we properly call 'good sense' or 'reason' -- is naturally equal in all men." René Descartes *(1596-1650); Discourse, Philosophical Writings of Descartes, trans. J. Cottingham, R. Stoothoff and D. Murdoch, I. p. 111*

". . . amongst men, there are very many, that think themselves wiser, and abler to govern the public, better than the rest; and these strive to reform and innovate, one this way, another that way; and thereby bring it into distraction and civil war." Thomas Hobbes *(1588-1679); Leviathan, English Works, 3, p. 51*

"All our knowledge falls within the bounds of possible experience." Immanuel Kant *(1724-1804); Critique of Pure Reason, trans. N. Kemp Smith, A 134/B 173*

Where individuals have not yet demonstrated voting awareness, or otherwise require the services of a parent or guardian, a parent or guardian is responsible for completing the individual's return and remitting the appropriate Life Security payment and tax.

There are four categories of government programs.

Basic Federal Services are those services which provide the stable, predictable environment which is central to freedom in a democratic society. They could include: parliament, justice, police, defense, monetary system, immigration, environment, communicable disease, taxation, and annual reporting. These basic services will be provided without reference to resident approval because they represent the essential ingredients of a stable, democratic environment and are the legitimate focus of representation by population government.

Federal Non-basic Programs include those services which the elected representatives have passed, and where more than 50% of the residents in Canada have indicated within the last year they both approve of the program, and have paid a budgeted equal amount necessary to balance the budget for that program. Recurring programs are expected at the provincial and municipal levels. The federal non-basic programs are the least likely to survive because they will only be funded by taxes paid by individuals after Life Security, Basic Federal Services, Municipal taxes, and Provincial taxes have been funded.

Fading Programs include those services which the elected representatives have passed, and where the program has previously been a non-basic commitment (recurring program), and where at least 50% of the residents have indicated within the last year they do not approve of the program. Fading programs are expected at all three government levels until sanity returns.

Emerging Programs include those programs which the elected representatives have passed, but where at least 50% of the residents have not yet indicated they approve of the program. Emerging programs are expected at the provincial and municipal levels. Emerging programs at the federal level are unlikely because the funding issues are formidable.

Critical to a democracy is the premise every informed citizen has a vote. Also critical to a democracy is the need to ensure a vote carries with it a responsibility to share equally in the obligations inherent in the items voted upon. Canada has ignored the responsibility aspect of democracy and has reached the point where governments are stealing from the minority and spending funds which they do not have. Both of these are immoral and, if done individually, illegal.

We must align government expenditures with democratic responsibility, and ability, to pay.

The democratic responsibility to pay can be established by the approval of the majority of residents who pay an equal amount required to balance the estimated budget.

The ability of the majority to pay must be established by a rational formula. I suggest every resident individual should have individual obligations for life security and government funding commensurate with ability to pay.

Chapter 3 Individual Obligations

No individual shall pay more tax than the majority of individuals in the jurisdiction pay. One of the Ten Commandments is "Thou shalt not steal." Many good-hearted individuals would never dream of stealing a candy bar, but encourage governments to steal money from wealthier individuals. How often have you heard "force the rich to pay their fair share?" It is a strange definition of "fair" that says the majority can steal from the wealthy because the wealthy are a minority.

A 1909 Supreme Court of Ontario judgment ruled "the prohibition, thou shalt not steal, has no legal force upon the sovereign body." What a travesty. How many otherwise rational people agree the state should be allowed to plunder at will? Too many in Canada. I hope to reduce the number.

If two people gang up on a third person and steal his money, we all agree that is theft. If the same two people walk into a polling booth and vote to steal the third person's money; that is democracy! Does that make the two-sided polling booth twofaced? Will you allow a degree of rationality to seep to the surface?

Many Canadians believe the tax system needs to be changed and simplified. This book introduces fundamental changes in the tax system which could lead to real democracy; which has been decaying in Canada for many decades.

Every resident will submit an Individual Obligations return on or before the anniversary of his or her birthdate. The annual return will be limited to the digital equivalent of one side of one 8.5" x 11" page.

We must align government expenditures with democratic responsibility, and ability, to pay.

The democratic responsibility to pay can be established by the approval of the majority of residents who pay an equal amount required to balance the estimated budget.

The ability of the majority to pay must be established by a rational formula.

Tax Administration

Every federal, provincial, and municipal government will maintain a central computer database which will be updated immediately after the last day of each month. These databases will include the data relevant for the following month's returns.

Any individual shall have access to the computer database (not individual taxpayer information) and shall be able to generate a return to be electronically filed.

Every federal, provincial, and municipal government will have a computer facility capable of recording the results in terms of tax collected and approvals of programs.

Taxes not remitted on time will incur a penalty of 2% per month, compounded monthly, and calculated on the actual number of days outstanding.

The collection efforts shall be those permitted to all unsecured creditors under Canadian laws.

No business shall be responsible for reporting to any government the income paid to Canadian resident individuals nor corporations. However, businesses shall report to individuals the income paid to those individuals and shall keep adequate records to permit efficient field reviews.

No business shall be responsible for withholding nor remitting amounts to the government with respect to the taxes of resident employees or other residents.

Individual Obligations

Where individual taxpayers wish to periodically accumulate funds to pay their actual taxes on or before their birthdays, they shall make such arrangements outside of all government bureaucracies.

The communication of government activities and operating results is inadequate. A database containing adequate published information will be available to any computer installation capable of internet communication. No government will print any hard copies.

Present government databases already list all individuals as to birth, immigration, death, and emigration. Virtually every Canadian resident eventually gets a "social insurance number".

The avalanche of data presently provided by individual and corporate taxpayers would be reduced dramatically.

The administration of the present tax system would be reduced by a phenomenal amount.

The indiscriminate printing and issuing of budget documents in two languages would stop.

Imagine the entire individual obligations for every individual, for every government level anywhere in the country, embodied in a 767 word document as follows.

A Canadian Individual Obligations Act

1 Every resident individual shall file a digital four segment return on the anniversary of his or her birthdate. Individuals under the care of a parent or guardian shall have their returns filed by a parent or guardian. The four pages in the return shall consist of an individual obligations return, a municipal approval form, a provincial approval form, and a federal approval form. The approval forms shall be those relevant to the jurisdictions containing the primary address of the individual.

2 By 5:30 a.m., Newfoundland time, on the first day of every month, every federal, provincial, and municipal government shall post the status and budgeted equal cost of every program

27

administered by them in the one-page approval form for that jurisdiction.

3 By 5:30 a.m., Newfoundland time, on every January 1, the federal government shall post the target Life Security Plan amounts for that calendar year for individuals from birth to age 110 and the personal exemption amount for the year.

4 Every approval form shall indicate approval or disapproval of the listed programs by the individual (or parent or guardian). The budgeted equal cost of the approved programs shall not exceed the tax remitted for that jurisdiction on any approval form. Where less than 50% of the total population in the jurisdiction indicates funded approval for a program, the program shall be designated as "fading" and shall be rationally phased out after 12 consecutive months of not receiving the funded approval of at least 50% of the individuals in the jurisdiction having birthdays in those 12 consecutive months. No emerging program shall be implemented until 50% of the individuals in the jurisdiction having birthdays in those 12 consecutive months have indicated approval of the program.

5 The individual's annual obligation shall be calculated as follows: a) the household income divided by the number of individuals in the household; b) the resulting average income per individual in the household shall be reduced by the personal exemption amount; c) the amount calculated in b) shall be divided by two. The result is the maximum individual obligation to contribute to the individual's Life Security Plan and to all levels of government.

6 Household income shall be the amount earned in the most recent calendar year ending at least three months prior to the current anniversary of the individual's birthday. Income shall be the amount established under generally accepted accounting principles in Canada.

7 Amounts (which would be included in income if the recipient were a Canadian resident) to be allocated to non-residents (including individuals) will have the tax treaty amount withheld by the payor and remitted monthly to the federal government. Where no tax treaty, 25% shall be withheld and remitted monthly to the federal government.

8 Interest rates applicable to past-due taxes and penalties shall be 2% per month, compounded monthly and calculated on the actual number of days outstanding. Tax collection efforts shall be those permitted to all unsecured creditors under Canadian laws and shall extend to all members of the household included in the annual returns.

9 Any government may request an independent review of the tax returns of any household so long as no more than one requested review is undertaken for any one calendar year, and so long as the government requesting the independent review advances $5,000 (plus consumer price index changes since 2002) in trust to the household's choice of financial institution. Such review must be requested within three years of the date the return was due. Where household income is increased as a result of such review, the household individuals shall remit, within 30 days, double the increased amount of tax due to each of the governments, plus 2% interest compounded monthly for the time period since the tax was originally due. Where household income is decreased as a result of such review, the government requesting the review shall remit, within 30 days, double the decreased amount of tax due to all Canadian governments, plus 2% interest compounded monthly for the time period since the tax was originally due. Where the requested review engagement report is provided by an accredited accounting firm for less than the $5,000 (plus consumer price index changes since 2002), the household shall receive the remaining amount in cash. Any appeal of taxes arising out of a requested review engagement report shall be through the regular civil arbitration and court system.

10 Failure to file a personal return on time shall incur a $1,000 (plus consumer price index changes since 2002) penalty. Such penalty shall double for each subsequent failure to file.

Toward Improving Canada

Individual Obligations Return

Name	Sarah Singlots	
Address	123 - 456 Street	
	SomeTown, SomeProv, A1B 2C3	
Sin#	123456789	
Birthdate	26-Jul-52	
Filing date	26-Jul-00	

Household income

Name	SIN #	Income
Sarah Singlots	123456789	70,000
Sammy Singlots	234567890	30,000
Serena Singlots	345678901	14,000
		114,000

Average income in household	38,000
Individual exemption	(21,500)
	16,500

Maximum individual obligation	**8,250**

Life security plan

Birthdate	26-Jul-52
Age in years	48
Target life security balance	262,000
Present balance in life security plan	(259,500)

Remittance to life security plan	**2,500**

Government remittances	Per Capita	Maximum	
Federal basic (x 1.4)	1,000	2,000	**2,000**
Municipal	1,000	2,000	**2,000**
Provincial	2,333	4,666	**1,750**
Federal non-basic	6,000	12,000	**0**
		20,666	0

30

In the fifth last line of the above example, the federal basic remittance is calculated at 1.4 times the per capita basic federal costs. This assumes the personal exemption is less than the median income of all individuals in the country. This should cause more than 50% of the population to pay tax and the federal basic tax is paid first; so the example assumes enough individuals will pay the federal basic tax to justify the factor of 1.4 instead of the 2.0 used to estimate the tax for the highest earning 50% of the population.

Municipal Integration

The effort expended, across the nation, to establish property values and collect property taxes and business taxes is a tragedy. It bears no relationship to the goods and services provided to the entities being taxed. Wouldn't it be simpler and fairer to calculate the municipal tax on the same tax base used by the federal and provincial governments? A base carefully designed to reflect responsibility, and ability, to pay. The base is already calculated. There is no need for a new set of judgments about the values of various properties and the colour of your toothbrush.

Why is there a business tax? The only real generator of wealth is independent enterprise. Businesses organize, provide jobs, provide structure, provide leadership, provide initiative, and provide enthusiasm. What does the municipality do? It taxes the business! The more you do for the municipality, the more it taxes you. This is akin to monitoring the kids in a class and beating on the best student whenever she shows good results.

Individuals have a hierarchy of needs funded by their income: home, food, clothing, child care, transportation, utilities, funding of their Life Security Plans, and funding of government services.

The integration of the municipal tax base with the federal and provincial tax bases allows simplicity and consistency. There's no need to debate social engineering, whether you are

Catholic or Protestant, whether your toilet faces south. The individuals in the household pay tax on the basis of responsibility and ability to pay.

There is a maximum of tax any one individual would pay. That maximum is the amount the top earning 50% of the people in the jurisdiction pay. No individual will be forced to pay more municipal tax than the top earning 50% of the people in the municipality pay. This means the majority in the municipality cannot steal from the high income individual (who is in a minority). This reflects Strand 3 of the fence which circumscribes the authority of our Alderpersons and Counsellors.

The municipal approval form lists the municipal programs on a line-by-line basis and shows the budgeted cost per individual of each of the programs. The individual cannot vote for more programs than she submits tax money to cover her per capita share of the programs. This reflects Strands 1 and 2 of the fence which circumscribes the authority of our Alderpersons/Counsellors. No Municipality will have more municipal programs than approved, and paid for, by more than 50% of the residents of that municipality. Under this model, do you believe any municipalities would continue to fund the International Paper Mache Contest for Left-Handed Arsonists?

Individual Obligations

Name	Sarah Singlots
Address	123 - 456 Street
	Somewhere, SomeProv, A1B 2C3
Sin#	123456789
Birthdate	26-Jul-52
Filing date	26-Jul-00

Emerging Programs	Per Capita	Yes or No	
Painting seasonal hoar frost on posts	86	No	
Matching shoe laces for village workers	2	No	

Recurring Programs	Per capita	Yes/No	Supported
Roads and sidewalks	200	Yes	200
Parks	120	No	
Policing	189	Yes	189
Taxation	12	Yes	12
Annual reporting	4	Yes	4
City council	10	Yes	10
Culture	1	No	
Education	154	No	
Fading Programs			
Recreation	18		
Sports	26		
Torism	15		
Business incentives	12		
Junkets	11		
Capital projects	5		
Water and sewer	45		
Electricity	116		
Natural gas	1		
Disaster assistance	10		
Public transit	51		
	1000		415

Unapproved municipal amount	585

Municipal per capita amount	1000

Provincial Integration

One may question the need for provincial governments in Canada. But this book focuses on proposals that can be implemented with little or no tinkering with the Constitution. Governments get blurred vision when they try to do more with the tax system than raise funds. You cannot have sin taxes, consumption taxes, and all the other forms of taxes without picking winners and losers. Governments must be even-handed. Therefore, the provinces will utilize the tax base used by all levels of government.

There will be no provincial sales taxes.

There will be no hotel room taxes.

Individuals have a hierarchy of needs funded by their income: home, food, clothing, child care, transportation, utilities, funding of their Life Security Plans, and funding of government services.

The integration of the provincial tax base with all other government levels allows simplicity and consistency. There is no need to debate social engineering or mood swings.

There is a maximum of tax any one individual would pay. That maximum is the amount the top earning 50% of the people in the jurisdiction pay. No individual will be forced to pay more provincial tax than the top earning 50% of the people in the province pay. This means the majority in the province cannot steal from the high income individual (who is in a minority). This reflects Strand 3 of the fence which circumscribes the authority of our members of the Legislative Assemblies.

The provincial approval form lists the provincial programs on a line-by-line basis and shows the budgeted cost per individual of each of the programs. The individual cannot vote for more programs than she submits tax money to cover her share of the programs. This reflects Strands 1 and 2 of the fence which circumscribes the authority of our members of the Legislative Assemblies. No province will have more provincial programs than approved and paid for by more than 50% of the residents of that province. How sweet it is!

Individual Obligations

Provincial Approval Form

Name	Sarah Singlots
Address	123 - 456 Street
	SomeTown, SomeProv, A1B 2C3
Sin#	123456789
Birthdate	26-Jul-52
Filing date	26-Jul-00

Emerging Programs	Per Capita	Yes or No	
Dress up the politicians program	145	No	
Pinto squirrel habitat endowment	16	No	

Recurring Programs	Per Capita	Yes or No	Supported
Welfare for the truly needy	230	Yes	230
Medicare for the truly needy	300	Yes	300
Education	800	Yes	800
Ground transportation	180	No	
Air transportation	80	No	
Legislature	3	Yes	3
Annual reporting	4	Yes	4
Provincial parks	35	Yes	35
Taxation	10	Yes	10
Clean air	3	Yes	3
Clean water	2	Yes	2
Natural resource regulation	5	Yes	5
Civil court system	10	Yes	10
Correctional services	25	Yes	25
Fading Programs			
Agriculture	2	No	
Housing	3	No	
Economic development	1	No	
Sports and recreation	1	No	
Culture	1	No	
Disaster assistance	2	No	
Support for aboriginals	1	No	
Workers' compensation board	2	No	
Hospital funding	3	No	
Child and family support	2	No	
Tourism promotion	2	No	
Business incentives	1	No	
Crown corporations	5	No	
Universal medicare (except needy)	1	No	
Ubiversal welfare (except beedy)	1	No	
Debt servicing	618	No	
	2,333		1,427
Unapproved provincial amount			906
Municipal per capita amount			2,333

35

Federal Integration

The basic services involved in a democratic country must be met. In order to fund these basic elements, the first segment of tax paid by any individual will be the amount prescribed by the federal government under our system of electing Members of Parliament and approval by Senators. However, historical government involvement has been continually expanded and abused by every federal government. Therefore, after the truly basic services have been funded, the municipal and provincial governments shall get first access to discretionary programs. This leaves discretionary federal programs as the least likely to be funded by more than 50% of the residents of the country. This is rational because it is difficult to design discretionary programs suitable for the disparate populations of a diverse country. There will be no transfer payments from one level of government to another. Governments will not pick winners and losers. Individual responsibility will be the guiding parameter.

The federal government will have access to all corporate tax. However, corporate tax planning is expected to reduce corporate tax to a nominal amount. Non-resident taxes will accrue to the federal government.

Governments must be even-handed. Therefore, the federal government will utilize the tax base used by all levels of government.

There will be no more Goods and Services taxes.

There will be no more Canada Pension Plan premiums.

There will be no more Employment Insurance Plan premiums.

There will be no more charity deductions or charades.

There will be no more nuances. The entire Individual Obligations mandate will be contained in the 749 word Individual Obligations Act.

Individuals have a hierarchy of needs funded by their income: home, food, clothing, child care, transportation, utilities, funding of their Life Security Plans, and funding of government services.

The integration of the federal tax base with all other government levels allows simplicity and consistency. There's no need to debate social engineering, or mood swings. There is a maximum of tax any one individual would pay. No individual will be forced to pay more federal tax than the top earning 50% of the federal population. This means the majority in the country cannot steal from the high income individual (who is in a minority). This reflects Strand 3 of the fence which circumscribes the authority of our Members of Parliament.

The federal approval form lists the federal non-basic programs on a line-by-line basis and shows the budgeted cost per individual of each of the programs. The individual cannot vote for more programs than she submits tax money to cover her share of the programs. This reflects Strands 1 and 2 of the fence which circumscribes the authority of our Members of Parliament. The federal government will have no more non-basic programs than approved and paid for by more than 50% of the residents of the country. Fresh air!

Toward Improving Canada

Name	Sarah Singlots
Address	123 - 456 Street
	Somewhere, SomeProv, A1B 2C3
Sin#	123456789
Birthdate	26-Jul-52
Filing date	26-Jul-00

Emerging Programs	Per Capita	Yes or No	
Daycare	189	No	
Job creation	251	No	

Recurring Non-Basic Programs	Per capita	Yes/No	Supported
Finance	418	Yes	418
External affairs	182	Yes	182
Transport	166	No	
Public works	166	No	
Veterans' affairs	91	Yes	91
Privy council	3	Yes	2
Governor General	2	Yes	3
Fading Programs			
Health	660	No	
Welfare	660	No	
Employment	706	No	
Indian affairs	150	No	
Northern development	27	No	
Industry, science, technology	139	No	
Communications	96	No	
Secretary of Sate	202	No	
Statistics Canada	29	No	
Energy, mines, resources	75	No	
Fisheries and oceans	37	No	
Supplies and services	32	No	
Atlantic Canada	21	No	
Western Canada Diversification	16	No	
Labour	11	No	
Forestry	11	No	
Consumer and corporate affairs	11	No	
Debt servicing	2,089	No	
	6,000		696

Unapproved federal amount	5,304

Federal discretionary per capita amount	6,000

Chapter 4 Corporate Tax

The concept of corporate tax, of any kind, violates the democratic ideal in that one vehicle that marshals resources is treated differently than other vehicles such as partnerships, unincorporated joint ventures, and proprietorships. However, there is an entrenched mindset "expecting" corporations to be taxed. Corporations do achieve limited liability for individual investors and have, traditionally, not had the income automatically flow through to the shareholders for income tax purposes.

Corporate income tax policy will be changed to include the following: the tax rate will be 50% of the net increase in retained earnings before the tax, but after payment of dividends. Retained earnings to be the amount established under generally accepted accounting principles. The 50% rate is high enough to prevent shareholders from undertaking tax sheltering maneuvers by leaving taxable income in the company instead of flowing it through to the individual shareholders; no tax refund will be paid if retained earnings have a net decrease. Corporate taxes will again be due when retained earnings next exceed the retained earnings on which taxes were last paid; any amounts paid or payable to non-residents (which would be included in income if the recipient were a Canadian resident) will have the tax treaty amount withheld by the payor and remitted monthly to the federal government. Where no tax treaty, 25% shall be withheld and remitted monthly to the federal government, and corporate income tax is due on the anniversary date of incorporation and will be based on the most recent fiscal year ending at least three months prior to the anniversary date of incorporation.

This policy puts corporations on an equal footing with other business organizations and ensures non-residents currently pay a Canadian tax on profitable activity in Canada.

Every corporation shall be assigned an identification number at date of incorporation.

Canadian resident individuals will include their share of corporate income (which has not increased corporate retained earnings) in any calculations of household income.

The non-resident is ultimately responsible for the tax whether or not the tax was appropriately withheld at source.

Every Canadian resident individual or other entity is responsible for withholding the non-resident tax and remitting it monthly to the federal government.

Imagine the entire corporate tax obligation for every corporation, for every government level anywhere in the country, embodied in a 478 word document as follows.

A Corporate Tax Act

1 Every corporation shall file a tax return on or before the anniversary of its original incorporation date.

2 The tax rate shall be 50% of the net increase in retained earnings from the retained earnings on which taxes were last paid, before the tax, but after payment of dividends. Retained earnings to be the amount established under generally accepted accounting principles in Canada.

3 No tax refunds shall be paid if retained earnings have a net decrease. Corporate taxes shall again be due when retained earnings next exceed the retained earnings on which taxes were last paid.

4 Amounts (which would be included in income if the recipient were a Canadian resident) to be allocated to non-

residents (including individuals) will have the tax treaty amount withheld by the payor and remitted monthly to the federal government. Where no tax treaty, 25% shall be withheld and remitted monthly to the federal government.

5 Corporate income tax will be based on the most recent fiscal year ending at least three months prior to the anniversary date of original incorporation.

6 Interest rates applicable to past due taxes and penalties shall be 2% per month, compounded monthly and calculated on the actual number of days outstanding.

7 Tax collection efforts shall be those permitted to all unsecured creditors under Canadian laws.

8 Failure to file a corporate return on time shall incur a $1,000 penalty payable by each of the Directors. Such penalty shall double for each subsequent failure to file on time.

9 The federal government may request an independent review of the tax return of any corporation so long as the government advances $5,000 (plus consumer price index changes since 2015) in trust to the corporation's choice of financial institution. Such review must be requested within three years of the date the return was due. Where the corporation retained earnings (before tax) is increased as a result of such review, the corporation shall remit, within 30 days, double the increase in amount of tax due to the government, plus 2% interest compounded monthly for the time period since the tax was originally due. Where the corporation retained earnings (before tax) is decreased as a result of such review, the government shall remit, within 30 days, double the decrease in amount of tax due to the government, plus 2% interest compounded monthly for the time period since the tax was originally due. Where the requested review engagement report is provided by an accredited accounting firm for less than the $5,000 (plus consumer price index changes since 2015), the corporation shall receive the remaining amount in cash. Any appeal of taxes arising out of a *requested review engagement report shall be through the regular civil arbitration and court system.*

10 Every corporation's financial statements shall be reviewed or audited by an accredited accounting firm which is independent of the corporation, its directors, and its shareholders.

Corporate Tax Return

Company	Drive To Make A Buck Company
Suite and Street	123 - 456 Street
City and Province	Somewhere, SomeProv, A1B 2C3
Postal code	A1B 2C3
Business number	123456789
Incorporation date	April 17, 1998
Filing date	April 17, 2001
Fiscal year end	December 31, 2000

Cumulative income (loss) to prior year end before tax	180,000.00
Current income (loss) before tax	310,000.00
Cumulative income (loss) to current year end before tax	490,000.00
Cumulative dividends to prior year end	(90,000.00)
Current dividends	-
Cumulative dividends to current year end	(90,000.00)
Tax base	400,000.00
Cumulative tax at 50%	200,000.00
Less tax previously paid	(50,000.00)
Current tax to be remitted	150,000.00

Chapter 5 Questions and Answers

During the development of the life security, spending and tax ideas, several questions were raised. The questions and my answers follow:

Q: Why have you taken initiative in trying to change the Canadian political system?

A: It is discouraging to see a system penalize the producers and reward the failures. Not only is the cancer present, but it is spreading.

Q: Are you not concerned the "ordinary person" will get hurt?

A: There is no "ordinary person." There are only individuals. I believe it is fundamental each individual should take responsibility for his own life. When an individual reaches an intolerable set of circumstances, there are apparent ways to proceed: if the circumstances result in physical or mental inability to be self-supporting, then the Canadian way is to provide a reasonable environment, the cost of which is to be shared equally by a majority of residents; if the circumstances result in temporary inability to cope, such as in the case of a teenage single mother, a divorced parent with children, or a misguided lifestyle, then the individual has to make a serious decision, either, "I will adopt a path to regain or achieve self-sufficiency," or, "I will become a hermit."

No government can be expected to provide an acceptable lifestyle to an individual who will not take responsibility for his or her own life.

Toward Improving Canada

Where the individual makes a genuine commitment to regain or achieve self-sufficiency, then our social policies must be refined so the rewards are directly related to the individual's progress toward self-sufficiency.

Where the individual fails to make a genuine commitment or fails to achieve reasonable progress toward self-sufficiency, the government will provide the barest level of support for food, clothing, shelter, and health care.

Q: With your plan, there could be massive unemployment as the government programs fade out of existence. Isn't this a ridiculous way to treat a large group of Canadians?

A: I do not think it is ridiculous. In fact, I think it is rational. Let me explain.

Logic says each program can be supplied in an efficient manner. Therefore, if someone wants the service, and it is efficient, it can be privatized without undue unemployment. However, if it is inefficient, or if few people want to pay a fair price for the service, we can't get rid of it fast enough.

If a program is found to have thin support, then rationalization is important. Calgary experienced a classic case of a large residential home-builder which failed during the recession in the early 1980's. Out of the ruins, several trades-people, supervisors, clerical staff, and the like found other avenues of endeavour. Some started their own businesses, some found other employment, some started families, and, presumably, some did not adapt. But the situation was rationalized and the vast majority of the individuals did take responsibility for their own lives and made the adjustments they considered appropriate. Government workers cover a wide range of ability, education, age, and motivation; however, they cannot be considered to be the "low end" of a cross-section of workers in Canada. Therefore, we assume they can be integrated into a rational system.

If the municipal, provincial, and federal approval forms indicated a high proportion of "fading" programs as soon as the

44

plan was implemented, then a rational transition policy might include the following: a total freeze on hiring any employees anywhere in any Canadian government; encouragement for employees in apparent fading programs to find other employment during the fading period; leveraged buy-out schemes for employees to privatize their programs where the financing is not provided, nor guaranteed, by any Canadian government; as a fallback position, the fading programs could stay fading longer than the suggested 12 months to the extent the total number of government employees does not fall faster than, say, 20% (annually) of the original number of government workers when the new plan was implemented.

Q: Canadians seem to have a particular soft-spot for the underdog. How does the plan accommodate this mentality?

A: I see the underdog in two lights. The most appealing is the underdog who is committed to improving his position. For this individual, the plan is infinitely superior to the present system which blind-sides initiative at every turn.

The least appealing underdog is the one who decides he is the recipient of every bad break. While many people are the victims of broken homes, irrational parents, government manipulation, and ineffective education, they must stop and say, "I am primarily responsible for my life from here forward." To the extent individuals will do that, the social systems can be targeted and will be supported by the majority of Canadians. This kind of social system does not take an army of bureaucrats, rather it will be most successful if the system integrates the individuals who need temporary support with people who already have the individual responsibility mentality. The least appealing underdog is the one who excels at tear-jerker stories for mass consumption.

Q: A favorite political tactic is to accuse opponents of a hidden agenda. What is your hidden agenda?

A: I have trouble getting one agenda in focus; let alone a hidden one! I wish to present the complete, straight goods. Throughout the development of this plan, and the decisions to present it to the public, there were recurrent suggestions to piecemeal it and "manage" the public. I do not like that strategy. I want to present what I think is a rational, sane, bold initiative for Canadians and address each concern as it surfaces. While my personal philosophy is libertarian, I do not object to government programs supported consciously and funded equally by a majority of Canadians.

Q: The plan seems to fly in the face of the New Democrats' platform. Do you think the general public will accept your plan?

A: A majority of the New Democrats' "common people" are the very individuals who will indicate they do not want the program(s) or, at least, they don't want to pay for the program(s).

Q: The media should have a field day with the plan. You say it is "bold" and "rational". They might say it is "stupid," "naive, "does away with a hundred years of progress," "puts desperate mothers on the street," and many other things which could defeat the plan. How do you react to the potential for mass media criticism?

A: I request the media consider the following suggestions: first, adopt a mindset that will allow them to analyze how to make the plan work, rather than how to destroy a good system; second, start preparing their reports early enough so they can absorb the thrust of the logic before praising or condemning it; third, ask for clarification if some element is of importance to their enquiry. I am willing to commit time to this project. I will try to clarify my points of view on the nuances anyone cares to raise; and, fourth, do not set out to cast me as a villain, nerd, hero, incompetent, well-meaning fool, heartless free-enterpriser, saboteur, or any other overstatement. Start out by viewing me as a concerned, rational Canadian.

I do expect some complimentary coverage.

Q: The existing recurring programs having to do with Old Age Security and the Canada Pension Plan are "sacred trusts" in the eyes of many Canadians. What comfort can individuals who have counted on these programs get from adopting the plan?

Question and Answers

A: I view the Old Age Security program as a contract with people who are well into their lifetimes. While they have not contributed separate amounts to the plan, they have contributed what was asked of them over their lifetimes. I see calculating the net present value of Old Age Security for each individual and issuing Special Canada Savings Bonds for that amount. These bonds would be used after all other Life Security Plan resources were used. To the extent any of the bonds were left at the individual's death, the bonds would be cancelled without compensation.

A similar policy should be adopted for contributors to the Canada Pension Plan, recognizing there is an element of provincial bonds inherent in the Canada Pension Plan arrangements. In my view, we can be relatively generous in our transition policies because there is an end in sight; the individuals involved have participated in the Canadian dream and that dream should not be shattered in the latter part of individuals' lives.

Medicare, unemployment insurance, and many other programs can generate high levels of emotion. Underneath the emotion, individuals will want to be assured they are not breaking a contract with neighbours who have legitimately counted on a given level of support. Individuals will want to be assured the programs committing them to expenditures for generations to come have some rational support and feasible expectation of adequate funding.

Q: Under the plan, it is probable many industry and regional incentives will fade. Will this put undue pressure on such segments as farming, exports, and research and development?

A: You have ventured into a mine-field! We get into the sacredness of the family farm, the conviction productive research and development only occurs when you waste lots of money, the observation some are better able to manipulate government officials than others, the conviction government caused the problems in the first place so government should fix the problems, the conviction politicians are better judges of how to

47

redistribute wealth than the decisions of individuals who generate that wealth; the list goes on.

I see the transition to the new plan involving at least the following elements: honouring all existing contractual obligations (or negotiating terminations); flatly refusing to enter into any new contractual commitments not evolved through the emerging category of the new plan; reducing present subsidy policies by the greater of 10% per annum from the base level, and the reduction evidenced by major international competitors (or their governments); and setting all marketing boards, pricing bodies, and insurance schemes free from government protection and control. No business shall be required by law to participate in any binding pricing or marketing scheme. However, every business shall be required to honour the terms of any contract the business has freely signed.

Through all of this, I believe we can be generous in our transition policies because there is a sunset on the horizon. The rhetoric that can be marshalled on this topic can be formidable and could wreck the implementation of the plan.

Q: The model appears to place more tax on younger folks because the annual amounts required to maintain their Life Security Plans may be less than for older folks. Is this a reasonable policy approach?

A: On the surface, it seems unreasonable because it causes young people who are also contending with first cars, first homes, and young families to contribute sums to government, while older folks with the same income would have a larger proportion of their obligations amount going to life security. But the model is an effective educator and it corresponds somewhat with the human life cycle. When you are young, you make lots of long-term commitments because you have health, enthusiasm, vision, and naiveté. It is good to educate young folks on the cost of government before they get older (and wiser). Life security becomes more of a focus as one reaches middle age and it is logical to allow more of one's income to be set aside for the risks that have more perceived imminence. The ability to pay criteria is still in place. Young folks would not be giving up a different proportion of their current disposable incomes, but they would be funding more current government and less current contributions to their own Life Security Plans.

Q: Your frankness is refreshing. Why do you think politicians appear devious?

A: Canadians have a split personality, media people included. We often hear of politicians being criticized for saying things that are true and need to be said. Instead of complimenting them for their integrity and forthrightness, we comment on how stupid they are for not hiding the facts and saying what they think the public wants to hear.

There is another factor, too. Most of us are afraid of failure. If we state our case too clearly, we are afraid we will not be able to recover if our case is proven wrong. Instead, we make small incremental changes which, if wrong, are not so dramatic.

The trouble with this approach is: things keep going wrong faster than our incremental fixes are happening; and none of the changes are dramatic enough to get people's attention. This is why so many people conclude "nothing can be done."

Q: There is some support for periodic referenda (commonly referred to as TEL's, which is short for taxation and expenditure limits, to provide legitimacy to government programs. Why have you advocated the approval form instead of periodic referenda?

A: One of the results of mass media is the overwhelming impact of points of view that are well-merchandised or popular in a short time period. This leads to significant lobby initiatives and sensational positions having undue impact on many individuals. This, in turn, leads to less rational decisions than the decisions made day-in, day-out by individuals as they fill in their annual returns on their birthdays. It is difficult for a lobby group to affect more than half of the people every day, forever. If they do influence many people on a consistent basis, the majority rules and real democracy works. Referenda, any periodic elections, tend to be popularity contests where the personality, appearance, and presence of the key players tend to overshadow the substance of the programs under discussion.

As a final consideration, referenda cost significant resources in money, time, and disruption. This is okay every four years to elect government representatives, but it is not okay for deciding lots of issues day-in, day-out.

Q: The plan puts considerable onus on each tax-filer to make informed decisions on what generic government programs to support. Is the "ordinary Canadian" capable of making those informed decisions?

A: There are no "ordinary Canadians; there are only individual Canadians. Each individual gets by with an existing level of education, public awareness, income, interest, apathy, and bias. If they don't care very much, they will make choices others would not make. But the plan prevents them from approving more programs than they fund by remitting their share of taxes to cover those programs. As generic programs, that have been mainstays, show up in the fading category; publicity will focus on the components within that generic category. Politicians and the media will discover which individual programs within the generic category will receive support and which ones won't. The government will make the changes required to segregate the popular programs from the unpopular ones. Under no circumstances should the approval form for each government extend to more than the digital equivalent one side of one 8.5" x 11" page.

Q: You have ranked the generic programs into four categories: basic, federal non-basic (recurring), fading, and emerging. Your plan is quite clear on the federal non-basic (recurring), fading, and emerging categories, but there are critical considerations involved in the "basic" programs. Could you comment on the criteria which make some programs basic?

Question and Answers

A: Once you get past the political rhetoric and editorials, you find Canadians believe in a "rational self-interest" mode where people generally "live and let live". We want to be assured our security of person and property is adequately protected. This involves a police and a justice system that protects each of us from force initiated by others. On an international scale, we want to be assured we have a defense system. We want to have a Parliament, a monetary system, and some ability to communicate with foreign states. I have not articulated the precise criteria that should be used to define the "basic" programs best suited to Canada. However, I believe we should concentrate on keeping the criteria stringent so the basic programs really are basic.

Q: With your obvious interest in sane government, why have you not been more prominent in an existing political party?

A: My recent business experience has provided exposure to government, lawyers, and sophisticated businessmen. Only recently have I convinced myself I have something useful to say. On a private basis, my partners, family, relatives, clients, and both friends have all grown weary of hearing my ideas. But they have been useful filters as they help refine the raw ore into something I am willing to expose to wider public review. Most people around me have resigned themselves to the view nothing can be done. This is most discouraging because these people are in a position to do something. I am ready and willing to take a more prominent role in public affairs.

Q: Given the continuing controversy over the goods and services tax and Quebec aspirations, how do you see the plan developing in the next year or two?

A: There is an opportunity this plan could capitalize upon if it gets popular support. Federal, provincial, and municipal leaders have said, "If you have a better alternative, let's hear it. To all governments, I am saying, "I have a better alternative and here it is."

Q: Do you have any quotes people may use to capsulize your philosophy?

A: Well, my basic philosophy is: "Individuals must be allowed to act according to their own minds unless they initiate force."

On a lighter note, three bits of advice I like are: "Never say 'whoa' in a bad place; if you lose the right to fail, you lose everything; and you can get anywhere from here."

Chapter 6 Jobs

I articulate jobs related suggestions consistent with my philosophy and approach to governance in Canada. There will be flaws. Many will propose improvements. I welcome full discussion with hope we can find solutions which build on individual responsibility.

A common refrain is, "there are no jobs." Lots of folks perceive there are no jobs. The reason they think so is they narrowly define what job they are looking for; in what neighbourhood, at what pay. This is not acceptable. When the primary obligation rests with the individual rather than the state, the individual will find a job somewhere, somehow, at some pay rate. It may not be ideal, but it will be better than the safety net because the proposed safety net will be way down at the survival level, not at the "don't hurt my dignity" level.

For any individual who has built up a Life Security Plan, job loss means the Life Security Plan can be eroded to provide cash flow until a new job is found. Individuals should recognize any erosion of the Life Security Plan will erode the amount of funds available in the future (or will need to be replaced). This assures many unemployed folks will quickly find a new job so their future well-being is better preserved. A few will erode their Life Security Plan, and trust in the compassion of others, but this is better than designing systems that encourage many folks to abuse the system.

The Life Security Plan would assemble large sums of savings across the Canadian population. This pool of funds would be available to fuel Canadian business through pressure to effectively invest the pool of savings. Such pressure would help independent enterprise find capital for growth. No individual or household will be able to borrow from any Life Security Plan nor direct the investments of Life Security Plan's. These lending and investment functions will be done by institutions independent of the holders of Life Security Plans.

There are impediments to job creation. The overall business environment would be significantly improved by the proposals in this book. One remaining impediment is the government protected ability for workers to shut down production. No entity should be forced to sign a contract and no entity should be prevented by law from procuring alternate sources of labour. It is fine for workers to organize into unions. It is fine for unions to bargain on behalf of their members. It is fine for businesses to voluntarily sign contracts with unions and/or union members. But it is not acceptable for businesses to be prevented from hiring non-union members whenever the union withholds services or fails to have a contract in place. This simple but profound change in labour law would dramatically improve the business climate in any province that chose to implement it.

Many folks assume organized labour (protected by law) is the primary driver in protecting the masses from big business. It is assumed big business would take over everything if unions were stripped of force. Business needs productive human resources; the individuals who merit extra compensation will receive extra compensation. Those who bring less skill, loyalty, motivation, and integrity to their work will lose ground. What could be fairer?

The Life Security Plan removes the need for workers' compensation schemes.

Emphasis on individual responsibility removes the need for, and desirability of, minimum wage laws.

Chapter 7 Education

I articulate education related suggestions consistent with my philosophy and approach to governance in Canada. There will be flaws. Many will propose improvements. I welcome full discussion with hope we can find solutions which build on individual responsibility.

Some well-educated people believe Canadian education needs more funding. They are wrong. It needs more results. To get more results, it needs more individual responsibility from students, teachers, and administrators. How can more individual responsibility be brought to bear? Same answers as in other human endeavors: engagement, competition, reward merit, keep knocking down hurdles. Make sure the most competent get rewarded; the less competent get less.

"It is not by wearing down into uniformity all that is individual in themselves, but by cultivating it and calling it forth, within the limits imposed by the rights and interests of others, that human beings become a noble and beautiful object of contemplation." John Stuart Mill (1806-1873); On Liberty, P. 266

Many students and their parents think school is hard. Kids learn easily. Let them explore and compete and reward results. Each Canadian baby should be issued 60 education vouchers. Each voucher would be good for three months of effective education and could be tendered anywhere in Canada. Assuming education is a provincial matter, the provinces must agree the vouchers will be acceptable anywhere in Canada. This means a Canadian could get 15 full years' education, which could mean roughly the same education as a Master's degree or a professional degree in all except medicine. But there should be strings attached. A student must achieve a competency level represented by one voucher before receiving the next voucher. Do not wait until the student is 22 and wasted his/her vouchers before instilling individual responsibility. Make it a part of life from birth.

Where a young person chooses not to attend school or fails school and goes on to some other endeavour, the remaining vouchers will remain available for potential use sometime later in life. When the 60 vouchers are used up, no government will provide any more education or retraining to that individual.

The vouchers should be legal tender at any school of the student's (or parent's/guardian's) choice as long as it results in the student achieving the competency level for that course. Uniform, nation-wide competency levels will subject the students to a specified level of performance independent of the school providing the instruction. This should not be limited to academic criteria. The full range of human involvement should be encouraged.

Education has been primarily a provincial responsibility with federal tinkering. I propose the federal government get completely out of education.

When immigrants enter the country, they will qualify for 60 vouchers even if they are mature and educated. Canada will make the commitment to provide 15 years of education to every person who chooses to become a Canadian citizen. However, immigrants will have some milestones to meet along the way: every immigrant must fund the Life Security Plan up to the Security Plan Index for that immigrant's age before being released into the Country; every immigrant shall receive no more than 20 education vouchers prior to earning full citizenship. The remaining 40 education vouchers will be issued as part of the citizenship ceremony; every immigrant shall proficiently speak,

Education

write, and understand the dominant language in the province of
primary residence before earning full citizenship.

Chapter 8 Immigration

I articulate immigration related suggestions consistent with my philosophy and approach to governance in Canada. There will be flaws. Many will propose improvements. I welcome full discussion with hope we can find solutions which build on individual responsibility.

What biases characterize the majority of Canadians when it comes to consideration of immigration policy? I postulate the majority of individuals consider the following:

How compassionate can the country afford to be?

How tolerant am I prepared to be?

How much hassle will the immigrant cause?

How much and how fast will the immigrants change the existing patterns in the community?

To the extent I can live with all that, I will allow any immigrant in.

But Canadians are predisposed to be fair to the underdog. We are susceptible to emotional and rhetorical charges of racism, bigotry, rednecks, and hard heartedness. How do we establish a sensible policy? I suggest: Canada will annually set a national immigration maximum; each municipality will annually set a municipal immigration maximum; Canada will maintain a first come, first served list of the aspiring immigrants. Those immigrants will be screened for communicable diseases, life threatening diseases, and criminal records; the aspiring immigrants will register as individuals or as a family; the aspiring immigrants will fund each of their Life Security Plans with the

Canadian dollars required for their relevant ages before being released in Canada; the aspiring immigrants will agree to settle in a municipality that has indicated a willingness to accept immigrants as long as that municipality's quota is not filled; the aspiring immigrants who agree to a municipality and then change their mind will go through a rigorous process before being allowed to relocate. Such process would involve: application to the present municipality for permission to move out; identification of a new municipality with remaining quota for immigrants; and application to the new municipality for permission to move in.

Ultimately, the immigrant has three choices: stay in the original municipality; find a willing new municipality; or leave Canada and get the remaining Life Security Plan funds (including interest) back.

The policy does not mention race, creed, education, career, gender, age, or anything else except commitment to a Life Security Plan and a lack of serious health issues and criminal records. Young people have a better immigration opportunity because their Life Security Plan amounts would not be as prohibitive. Any municipality that feels insecure about the level of immigrants in general or about the level of one race in their midst could merely reduce the municipal quota to zero and accept no more immigrants until the existing population stabilizes, changes its collective mind, or whatever.

How do political refugees or hardship cases get considered? It is obvious Canada cannot even-handedly accept all the world's alleged political refugees and hardship cases that could surface. My proposal is the first-come, first-served list is the only way to get immigration status in Canada. If you're not next on the list, you don't get in. Any other policy opens the door to abuse, misuse of power, corruption, admittance of rabble-rousers, and all the problems we Canadians find frustrating. A better contribution to solutions to world problems is the verbal (but not financial) encouragement of Canadian retirees to work among underdeveloped countries' people to demonstrate more effective ways to educate, farm, manufacture, and export. The growth of native knowledge from peasant, to pioneer, to business person is the only lasting way to improve the conditions of the masses in underdeveloped countries. Putting gobs of money, food, and drugs in the hands of governments and bureaucrats guarantees perpetual corruption and undemocratic power.

Chapter 9 Justice

I articulate justice related suggestions consistent with my philosophy and approach to governance in Canada. There will be flaws. Many will propose improvements. I welcome full discussion with hope we can find solutions which build on individual responsibility.

Most individuals have an acceptable view of fundamental justice. This view is characterized by: do unto others as you would have them do unto you; the Ten Commandments; and Desiderata.

My preferred view is individuals should be allowed to act according to their own minds unless they initiate force.

We have allowed our justice system to drift away from fundamental justice by acceding to time delays, political correctness, plea bargaining, and different rules for different segments. The solution is a "back to basics" approach where justice is evenly applied. This chapter outlines some of the ideas that might usually achieve fundamental justice.

The Criminal Justice Process

Underlying all justice is the principle of individual responsibility. Our system has allowed this principle to be eroded by such defenses as youth, insanity, blind rage, and drunkenness. None of these defenses are acceptable. If an individual commits a criminal offense, they must be held accountable. The only defense against a criminal charge should be innocence.

Justice takes too long. The Crown should have a strong criminal case before charging an individual, and then the case should be decided by the lower court within 90 days. Each appeal all the way to the Supreme Court shall be completed within 90 days. A routine criminal case, which could pass through three courts would be finalized in 270 days. I know lawyers, judges, investigators, and other observers will object to the time limits. My answer to them is "you abused the system to the point of exasperation, now mend your ways, get the job done expeditiously, and without petty wrangling." All the requests for psychological testing and other stonewalling tactics will not be effective if the emphasis is on guilt or innocence rather than state of mind. Why should neurotic criminals get more leeway than otherwise normal criminals?

Parole should be discontinued. The Courts have a range of sentences at their disposal. The Courts should expect the sentences will be served.

Custody

There is concern about the economic consequences of locking up large numbers of criminals. The costs of prisons have escalated because: the relative comfort of the prisoners is assured; the level of security requires physical infrastructure and high numbers of personnel; and the prisoners are not self-supporting.

Beyond the costs of operating prisons, there is a high price to pay for segregating couples, extended families, and normal living conditions.

The following custodial structure seeks to provide adequate public protection with economically feasible ways to incarcerate criminals.

The structure includes three levels of custody: minimum security, medium security, and maximum security. Judges would be responsible for picking the level of security as well as the length of confinement. There is significance to the level of security for the criminals because exit from the facility before the sentence expires results in an automatic move to a facility with the next higher level of security.

What do we do with the criminal who exits the maximum security facility before his/her sentence expires? Execute him/her. This is not capital punishment, this is damage control. It is one thing to commit one or more criminal offenses that lands an individual in the maximum security facility; it is quite another when that same individual, knowing the risks, exits that facility for any reason before completing the sentence. Execution of these types of individuals is not punishment; it is a necessary limit to the havoc we are willing to endure from one individual.

Many people believe a criminal with a long sentence (including a life sentence) will be more dangerous if they have no hope. This definition of hope relates to the hope of some existence outside the confines of an existing maximum security prison. The facilities envisioned in this new proposal are dramatically different.

A minimum security facility would be located near urban centres where the extended family could maintain contact. There would be individual housing units for each criminal and his/her immediate family. There would be garden plots, farm animals, and manufacturing plants, as developed by the criminals. There would be no alcoholic beverages, tobacco products, or hallucinogenic drugs allowed in the complex. The facility would be laid out in a pie shape where the "town square" and any business enterprises would be centred. Radiating out from the centre would be roads and paths leading to the individual residences.

The individual residences would have a minimum of facilities supplied by the government. Such minimum facilities would include concrete interior and exterior walls, floors and ceilings, with an insulated core, thermopane windows, and entrance door. The residence would have a common room and two bedrooms. No closets; no furniture; no cupboards; no carpet; no blinds; nothing but a wood burning cook stove. The residence would have a cellar which would contain a wood burning furnace, an ice house, and a root cellar. When a criminal first enters the facility, he/she would be allowed to live in a temporary residence for seven days to decide on career, location, facilities available, and status of garden plots. At the end of the seven days, the criminal may choose any unclaimed residence. From then on, he/she would be on his/her own; just like a pioneer. Individual responsibility is the guiding force. Prior to the exit of a criminal at the end of his/her sentence, the criminal may barter, give, or sell the assets built up to other inmates for whatever he/she can negotiate, recognizing the only temporary title holder permitted will be a criminal in the facility.

The individual living units would not have electricity, running water, or sewer. Instead, each group of residences would have a common facility which would include showers, toilets, wash basins, and laundry facilities. These facilities would be originally installed to high industrial standards. Day-to-day care and upkeep would be left to the local council. An adequate supply of clean water would be provided from federal government funds. While the washhouses would be supplied with electricity paid for by the federal government, there would be no access to government-funded electricity for the use of residents, beyond servicing the washhouses.

One might wonder how the meek or inept individual would make out in such a facility. The answer is the same as in ordinary society. There will always be an uneven distribution of skills, drive, intelligence, physical, and mental capacity. When the criminal hits bottom, the same level of subsistence support available to other citizens would be provided; no better, no worse. But such support would not be attractive to anybody who has any sense of individual responsibility.

Each criminal entering a minimum security facility would be fitted with an electronic monitor built into a permanent necklace.

Such electronic gizmo would be worn continuously from start to end of sentence. It will emit a traceable signal from a radius of, say, 100 miles from the location of any "receiver" and the location of the criminal will be known. The separation of the necklace from the criminal would trigger immediate emergency notice of the time and location of the separation. Existing police techniques would be used to locate and apprehend the criminal. Any violation of the security necklace or unauthorized exit off of the facility would result in automatic movement to a medium security facility.

Visitors and family members would be free to come and go at will from the facility. Any school age children living in the facility will be bussed to the nearest school(s) as appropriate.

The residents in the facility would make appropriate use of items salvaged from the community at large. Such materials as waste from renovations, waste from manufacturing and construction projects, and abandoned clothing, should be encouraged to be assembled by criminals who are proprietors of stores in the facility. Such proprietors could barter such materials for items or services they need or want. To the extent non-proprietor criminals can procure needed materials or services, these can be bartered to the proprietors or to other residents. Appropriate screening of incoming shipments will be designed to restrict the entry of alcohol, tobacco, drugs, and other banned items and substances.

Policing in the facility would be done by carefully selected Royal Canadian Mounted Police who have the combination of skills and personality to treat the criminals and other residents as humans and still maintain law and order.

The facility would be run by a democratically-elected Council of Residents (who may or may not be criminals). Within boundaries, the Council would have considerable authority. Such Council could deal with common washrooms, roads, noise, and community hall.

Similar guidelines would be in place for the medium security and maximum security facilities, but with enhanced levels of security as described below.

The medium-security facility would be enclosed by a fence that could not be scaled without access to physical facilities such as ladders, climbing ropes, or explosives. Electronic surveillance would be in place at all times and the gates to the facility would be arranged and manned to provide reasonable levels of protection from unauthorized exit of criminals. The criminals themselves would be fitted with an electronic surveillance gizmo on one ankle in addition to the necklace described in the minimum-security module. Same guidelines and rules apply. Any exit prior to completion of sentence will result in transfer to a maximum-security facility.

The maximum-security facility would be surrounded by a virtually impenetrable enclosure. The gates would be appropriately arranged and manned to detect criminals exiting the facility. In addition, each criminal incarcerated in the maximum security facility would be internally fitted with an electronic gizmo that would have two properties: it would allow the receiving of its signals for a radius of 1,000 miles and include the ability to establish the location of the criminal; and it would be immediately fatal to the criminal if the gizmo was removed without authorized, secret procedures under clinically acute care circumstances.

The result of exiting the maximum security facility before the end of sentence is automatic execution. This is not designed as a penalty; it is designed as ultimate control. The criminal would obey the maximum security guidelines or die. The advocates of hope will therefore be inclined to reinforce the opportunities within the maximum-security facility instead of systematically eroding the right of law-abiding individuals to be protected from proven high-risk criminals.

There will be those who are concerned about the well-being of spouses and children who accompany criminals into any of the facilities. The same rules of fundamental freedom and justice apply to such individuals whether they are in or out of a custodial facility. Physical or mental abuse will be treated the same. In some respects, the spouse will have more options because an abusive criminal spouse will be restricted in mobility, while the non-criminal spouse is free to live or go anywhere. On balance, the ability for criminals to live substantially self-supporting, useful lives while incarcerated outweighs the perceived risks to affected non-criminals who choose to associate with the criminals.

Civil Cases

There are relatively few who believe Canada's legal system provides efficient, appropriate civil decisions, promptly and cost effectively. Two primary villains contribute to the slow resolution of civil disputes. The worst villain is the extreme politeness and accommodation allowed to slow down the system. The second is the obsessive concern for getting all the relevant evidence. The result of these two situations is unacceptable delay between the launching of a lawsuit and the ultimate resolution of the case.

Here is my proposed solution. Every civil suit will be put to arbitration exactly nine weeks from the day the statement of claim was filed. The applicant will have up to one week to present the case; the respondent will have up to one week to present a defense; and the arbiter will have up to one week to provide a written ruling.

Any appeal of the arbiter's ruling must be filed within 13 weeks from the date the statement of claim was filed. The appeal will be heard starting exactly 22 weeks from the date the statement of claim was filed. The appellant will have up to one week to present the case; the respondent will have up to one week to present the defense; and the judge will have up to one week to provide a written ruling.

Any appeal will go through a similar process and be completed within 38 weeks from the date the statement of claim was filed.

Any appeal to the Supreme Court will go through the same process; so every civil suit will be resolved within 51 weeks, regardless of the number of appeals. The overwhelming majority of cases will be solved at arbitration and few will go beyond the first level of court proceedings.

What about costs of the process? Civil suits are often fought between combatants of unequal means. A combatant initiating an arbitration hearing shall pay $5,000 (adjusted by the Consumer Price Index) into trust. At the end of the arbitration process, the arbiter will order the deposit be paid to the winner.

Any appeal to the first level of court will be accompanied by a $10,000 deposit (adjusted by the Consumer Price Index) from the appellant. Such amount will be awarded to the winner of the appeal.

Any appeal to the second level of court will be accompanied by a $20,000 deposit (adjusted by the Consumer Price Index) from the appellant. Such amount will be awarded to the winner of the appeal.

Any attempted appeal to the Supreme Court will be accompanied by a $40,000 deposit (adjusted by the Consumer Price Index) paid by the appellant. Such amount will be paid to the respondent if the Supreme Court does not grant leave to appeal or issues a judgment in favour of the respondent. The appellant gets the deposit back if the judgment is in the appellant's favour.

While the arbiter's decisions will not be viewed as judicial precedents and will not be published, the Courts will take the decision of the arbiter as the key piece of reliable evidence. The appellant will be expected to provide convincing evidence the arbiter erred in the circumstances. The idea is to be sure all potential litigants take the arbitration process seriously.

Lawyers have a tendency to name peripheral parties in any claim in the hopes some "off the wall" argument will ultimately be useful or the hassle factor will lead to some favourable settlement. There must be tempering of this tendency. Therefore, the $5, $10, $20, and $40 thousand dollar rules will apply to every named party in a dispute. So, if a statement of claim names 10 parties, the aggressor is exposed to 10 times the $5, $10, $20, and $40 thousand dollar payments into trust. This is necessary to control the irresponsible dragging in of innocent parties. In addition, judges will be given leeway and encouragement to award cost recoveries to the unjustified naming of defendants to a claim.

In a similar vein, class action suits will always require the naming of the individual claimants in the class and those claimants will be exposed to the $5, $10, $20, and $40 thousand dollar deposits. The launching of civil suits will have a financial impact at the front end. In this way, contingent fee arrangements will be mitigated.

How do the above proposals affect a "little guy" who feels wronged by a bigger player? He better be sure he is working with provable facts, rather than emotion or pique. He will be expected to come up with $5,000 (adjusted by the Consumer Price Index) for a deposit for arbitration. Third, he needs to find an efficient and effective way to present his arbitration case. The community would quickly adapt to the needs of this kind of presentation and economical services would be available. The Courts would be instructed to rely heavily on the arbiter's decision. The little guy therefore has to win the arbitration hearing or face real stiff obligations in terms of proof and front-end funding for deposits and legal fees when he enters the civil court system.

The justice system is populated by too many lawyers. The legal profession presently provides drafts of laws, offense, defense, judge, appeal judge, and Supreme Court judge. What if the legal profession is wrong or out-of-step with fundamental justice? Wrongs are perpetuated and used as precedents. To reduce the influence of lawyers, the justice system will adopt two restrictions: no arbiters will be lawyers; and no provincial court judges will be lawyers.

In this manner, the first and third rungs of the civil justice system would be decided by rational people who are not steeped in the finer points of law, but are well-qualified to decide on fundamental justice. The second and fourth rungs would be populated by judges who are trained as lawyers and who could provide the traditional strengths of the common law system and careful second thought to the civil justice system. The Supreme Court would be expected to be loath to grant leave to appeal a decision that sided with the arbiter and the non-lawyer judge on the third rung of the system.

Chapter 10 Environment

I articulate environment related suggestions consistent with my philosophy and approach to governance in Canada. There will be flaws. Many will propose improvements. I welcome full discussion with hope we can find solutions which build on individual responsibility.

While my preferred structure is minimum government, there is a place for protection of the environment. In order to get a balance between property rights and others' rights, I envision a plane emanating from the centre of the earth to the end of space and passing through the earth's crust at property lines. To the extent a property owner can ensure pollutants do not leave the invisible planes mentioned above, the property owner can pollute to his heart's content. However, the instant he pollutes, or could pollute, any area outside the invisible planes, he is subject to stringent environmental requirements. The property owner must ensure air and water, outside controlled vessels, is clean. This is more stringent than industry now faces. Existing businesses should be monitored and forced to clean the air and water emissions to clean standards in, say, five years, without exception.

Here are my proposals for habitat, renewable resources and non-renewable resources:

First, publish a schedule for the development of a comprehensive environmental plan. For example, consider a two-year plan with the following elements:

Start with an invitation to every interested party to submit its suggestions for the areas under Canadian control that should be protected. This could have an eight-month time limit before the deadline for submissions;

A study group consisting of two members selected by each party that submitted a study (no matter how many) would then be organized into teams to digest and organize the various submissions into a coherent discussion document. Such document would have the following attributes:

Identify the key habitats for every species of animal and plant life acknowledged by the submissions;

Identify the cultural and historical areas acknowledged by the submissions;

Identify any pristine areas that have so far escaped significant human influence;

Identify a communication and transportation grid of roughly 300 kilometers in each direction throughout the country that could be utilized with minimal damage to surrounding habitat;

Present a tentative plan that would best provide for the enactment of protected areas of four types: 7% of the total Canadian area as pristine preserves which would be rigorously protected from all human intervention and development; 7% of the total Canadian area as federal parks which would be protected by the Canadian Federal Government; 7% of the area of each province which would be protected by the provincial governments; and 7% of the total Canadian area which would be protected by trusts administered by concerned individuals (entities) and dedicated to specific habitats, cultural settings, and historical settings.

Such discussion document to be ready in about eight months from launch date. This discussion document would then be available for submissions by all interested parties, including aboriginals, governments, industries, businesses, individuals, international nature groups, and environmentalists, with a view to assembling a feasible, comprehensive, significant environmental protection policy for Canada's land and water areas. Submissions would be accepted for about six months.

At the end of the submissions stage, an international body would be invited to rationalize all the submissions and recommend a final plan to the Federal Government. The Federal Government would then debate and accept a plan for Canada and recommend it to the provinces and territories for their debate and approval. One could visualize some entity like the National Geographic Society as being both interested and competent in assessing the submissions and recommending the final plan.

Inherent in all this would be an understanding the remaining 72% of the Canadian land base would be available for commercial exploitation. There may be room for regulatory control over renewable and non-renewable resources, but not the continual and irresponsible intervention of special interest groups presently allowed to ride roughshod over independent enterprise. The proposals in the Justice chapter will help to control intervention and speed up the civic process.

Issues will evolve from aboriginal land claims, private developments entrapped in proposed protected areas, and costs of swapping privately-held lands for Crown lands. My view is the longer we leave environmental issues to ad hoc decisions, the fewer realistic options will be left. Protection of 28% of the land and water area of Canada will put the country on the leading edge of environmental responsibility and we should get on with it before it is too late.

The communication and transportation corridors will also cause debate and concern. I propose a five mile-wide strip be included in the corridors with usage as follows: roads, pipelines, railways, power lines, and communication towers would be in the middle mile; the mile on each side of the middle mile would be available for private ownership and development of accommodation and recreation activities suitable to travelers and local demand; and the outside mile on each side would be a transition zone where there is no development, but people would not be restricted from hiking, swimming, and skiing. One of the challenges involved in corridors through protected areas is to ensure the relatively free movement of wild life. This raises the opportunity for creative ways to build highways below or above ground and other innovations to infringe as little as possible on nature.

Chapter 11 Welfare

I articulate welfare related suggestions consistent with my philosophy and approach to governance in Canada. There will be flaws. Many will propose improvements. I welcome full discussion with hope we can find solutions which build on individual responsibility.

There is often a substantial gap between what a person says he will do and what he actually will do. Common examples are: a co-worker agrees to purchase season's tickets to a professional team's home games. When it comes time to pay for the seats, the priorities have changed; a father readily offers to help his daughter with her homework all through the school year, but only helps her twice; a voter agrees no one should live below the poverty line, but then finds ways to avoid a pro rata share of taxes.

As a result, many high-minded ideals are implemented into law without questioning whether a majority of the residents wish to pay the costs on a pro rata basis.

In order to focus our policy decisions in a productive way, I propose the "crevice" theory. This theory postulates a person faces a series of crevices throughout a lifetime. Many of these crevices are well-known and are readily negotiated by the majority. Examples are: learning to walk; learning to talk; first day of school; first date; final exams; and marriage.

Other crevices have become formidable obstacles over the last half century. I believe these crevices have widened and deepened because individual responsibility has been eroded.

Toward Improving Canada

My policy suggestions have the following two main thrusts: improve the ability of individuals to confidently cross a variety of crevices and narrow several of the crevices which are too wide for many to cross.

One should recognize there will always be crevices. If we were able to eliminate all the known ones, people would invent a new set. A continuing quest to encourage individuals to acquire skills and confidence to cross identified crevices, as they become important to each individual, is a wholesome exercise.

This quest will have the best chance of success if we recognize human nature exists and build on natural tendencies, rather than on some utopian or naive vision of what society should look like. One should abandon such hallowed terms as: minimum wages, poverty line, universality, wage parity. All of these terms, and many more, lead individuals to believe someone else is responsible for their well-being. It is more productive to lead each individual to recognize he or she is individually responsible for well-being.

I grew up on a farm. Several times, I noticed the metamorphosis that occurred when the plow was put into use each season. The plow sat outside for several months and the mold board and shear rusted noticeably. When the plow was put to use, the first few rounds required extra power to pull the plow through the soil because of its rusty mold board. After a relatively few rounds, the mold board was a shiny, polished silver colour and was easier to pull through the soil. This seems to me to be a good analogy for what happens to individuals who are not using their individual responsibility mold boards. They get rusty. Then they want government to come along and use chemicals and emery cloth to clean up what should not have rusted in the first place.

The common storage for grain on the farms in our community was a 12' x 12' wooden granary. Often, these bins were built by inexperienced pioneers using whatever materials were available. Some of the granaries were structurally inadequate, so the pressure of the grain tended to push the walls out. To counteract this tendency, many bins had heavy wires strung across them about four feet off the floor. One set of wires went from side-to-side and another set from front-to-back. The wires were tightened by twisting a stick between the wires until the wires were taut and able to help counteract the pressure of the grain on the walls of the bin. This was an inexpensive, effective fix for a problem that needn't have developed in the first place. Many times I banged my knuckles, ribs and arms on the wires strung across where I was trying to shovel grain. This story symbolizes my suggested approach to managing the size of the crevices individuals might wish to cross. The first message is the structures we build should be strong enough to keep the crevices narrow enough to cross. The second message is we can use wires (twisted tight) to keep the existing crevices from widening further, while individuals cross with existing skills and confidence. There will be some banged knuckles and bruised ribs, but individuals will survive and persevere.

My proposals are built on individual responsibility. Are you willing to expect all individuals will take primary responsibility for themselves? If a majority is willing, we can build a better Canada. If not, we are doomed to a steady erosion of our freedom and productivity. The choice is open to us.

Catalysis

The economic underperformers who have not yet achieved a median funding required by the Life Security Plan and those who have chosen to default on individual responsibility may have landed in their present predicament through various misfortunes such as poor upbringing, teenage pregnancy, misspent youth, immaturity, laziness, physical abuse, mental abuse, ad infinitum. This book proposes the catalysis model to help folks who could benefit from a leg up.

Catalysis, as used here, means a combination of specific analysis of the needs and wants of the target individual, and the identification of an appropriate mentor as a catalyst to help the target get from the present circumstances to individual independence.

The steps in the Catalysis process are: an individual asks for help from the village; the individual is encouraged to identify an appropriate catalyst; the catalyst and the individual mutually develop a contract (plan) to achieve financial independence within a reasonable timeframe (say five years), and cover basic food, clothing, and shelter immediately.

All of this is accomplished outside of any level of government. It reopens a meaningful role for churches, service clubs, individuals, business people, and neighbours;

Because this catalysis process is done completely outside of government, a myriad of ad hoc programs will be tried. Successful programs will be copied. Unsuccessful programs will atrophy. The whole range of community groups will regain meaning. Results will be positive and reinforced. Peer pressure will reinforce the program. Presumably, unacceptable environments will be reduced because abused spouses will have an avenue to escape; children will be put in healthier atmospheres; expectations will be raised; hope will be present;

There will be the usual naysayers who harp about two-tier systems; who worry about inappropriate catalysts; who fear change of any style. My answer to them is, "The present system isn't working and any general government program is doomed to fail. Why not focus on the individual? Isn't that rational?"

The risks to those who fall into a category of needing help through categories 3 and 4 are great. The remaining safety net for these folks (after the Life Security Plan is used up) will be way below most people's comfort level. There will be some transitional heartache and disasters because many will believe the safety net will not be lowered way below most people's comfort levels. Over a few years, the recognition individual responsibility is the norm will have a profound, positive effect on the wellbeing of the nation and its individual residents.

Hearken back to the taker-maker analogy. As soon as that blob of humans between the two backstops is tipped slightly toward the maker end, the whole blob gravitates to the maker end. My bias is the heavier the maker end becomes, the stronger the society. Those individuals who continue to hold collectivist philosophies will continue to merchandise alternatives.

I routinely work with owner-managers of businesses. It is my conviction individuals in businesses will enthusiastically adopt the philosophies and programs expounded in this book. Even the most paranoid members of our society will be astounded at the positive activity generated throughout Canada under a rational regime involving the approaches prescribed here.

It surprises me any responsible person would advocate people should receive welfare with dignity. To me, accepting welfare is the antithesis of dignity. Shouldn't people learn dignity from birth? Don't turn your food bowl upside down; accept toilet training; don't raise a consistent ruckus in public places; don't disrupt the school class; don't play Bridge full-time in university; don't collect employment insurance as a regular part of existence; don't be promiscuous; don't beg. The list could go on. Asking for government help is not dignified, should never be merchandised as dignified, and should not be legislated as dignified.

If an individual finds himself in a position where he needs to ask for help, then he should make a personal commitment he will do everything in his power to avoid asking for future help, and should wholeheartedly pursue a route to individual independence. Even though the indignity of asking for help is a blow, the dedicated efforts to learn from the underlying mistakes should insulate oneself from future setbacks. Genuine pursuit of individual responsibility will quickly demonstrate to the neighbours the helping hand was justified. A close analogy to the person asking for help is the maturing process of a teenager. Each teenager chooses a way to test the limits of acceptable behaviour as measured by parents, teachers, church, community, and police. To the extent neither the teenager nor the authorities around him provide acceptable limits, a life is wasted. In the adult world, our welfare system has encouraged the irresponsibility of the individuals who apply for welfare. I seek to establish some rational limits that will allow the vast majority of potential welfare recipients to choose to be short-term partakers.

What path might an individual choose if he decides to ask for welfare? His first line of attack should be his personal initiative, his education vouchers, his Life Security Plan, his family (close and extended), and his friends. If this whole range of support systems proves inadequate, then the individual has two broad choices: he can ask for formal help with the understanding help will come with a genuine commitment from the applicant to become individually responsible within a relatively short time; or he can decide to lead a life of mere subsistence.

The person who admits he needs help and makes a genuine commitment to rapidly improve to self-sufficiency will find an array of community resources available to help him. The path he chooses will depend on the following factors: what support structures are known to be available in the community; what sponsor group is most consistent with the individual's personal preferences and career interests; what education vouchers remain to be used what help the family and friends will provide once the individual demonstrates a willingness to become individually responsible and financially independent; and the catalyst he chooses to provide the guidance, stability, maturity, street smarts, and understanding to get the person on a path leading to individual responsibility and financial independence.

Once the support structure and catalyst have been located, all the parties will develop a written contract which will spell out the benefits and the obligations of all the signatories. In the circumstances, the applicant is the most vulnerable for several reasons: it may be a life and death attempt to get ahead; it may be

Welfare

past experience shows "nobody cares;" and it may be the sponsor groups and catalysts do not adequately perform their functions. This means there will be failures. It also means all the parties will hear of circumstances that worked well or went badly awry. An evolution will take place where several approaches will emerge, probably including: individuals will struggle along without getting involved in any formal process; individuals, churches, service groups, and business groups will refine their programs so the likelihood of successful fulfillment of the programs will be improved; individuals will recognize the consequences of ignoring education, stealing cars, getting pregnant, divorcing, quitting jobs, and other choices could result in genuine pain. Prudence will emerge across the spectrum. Wouldn't that be a welcome development?

There might be a tendency for individuals to eke a living out of panhandling and street vending. Canadians generally do not accept panhandling and street vending so this type of activity would have to be met with enough obstacles to make it unacceptable as an alternative to committing to an effective plan to gain individual responsibility and financial independence.

The individual might choose a life of mere subsistence. We can have a debate over what mere subsistence means, but my definition would include enough funds to buy salt, flour, and other basics, but not enough to buy liquor, cigarettes, or drugs. The media mentions "smart cards" for various commercial and healthcare monitoring plans. Perhaps a smart card could be issued annually to an individual seeking subsistence welfare. This smart card would allow commercial vendors to issue goods and services having a cumulative daily value of, say, $2. The recipient would not be allowed to bank two or more days' worth of purchases so he could buy a bottle of liquor for, say, $10. Each day he would be allowed to purchase $2 worth of merchandise. Presumably, merchants could invent ways to group several $2 for the recipient to buy staples, but the size of the transactions would make the hassle to the merchant unattractive as a normal business practice, and it would only be done for regular, reliable recipients. Some experience in practice would soon establish the size of the daily amount that would keep the recipients alive with no frills. The goal is to make the mere subsistence option unacceptable to the masses.

Crevice Crews

Effective help for an individual has to be one-on-one. That is why governments and big businesses are not suitable vehicles for effective social assistance. The Catalysis model illustrates how individuals could get help. In an effort to find adequate words to help people conceptualize the individual obligations and help proposal, I suggest a "Crevice Crew", which will be dedicated to the attainment of individual responsibility by one individual (or one household).

A Crevice Crew could be one person, but it is more likely to be a family which is committed, as a family, to help the individual (household) wanting help. Notice I said "wanting," not needing. Most of us "need" help; only a small minority "want" help. No matter how much anyone "needs" help, I don't "want" to provide help unless the target genuinely "wants" help. The distinction is important. It will save us all a lot of grief.

How will the Crevice Crew work? There will be few rules and little structure. The guidelines will be something like this: an individual (or head of household) places his/her situation on a list of folks wanting help (this individual shall be called a "Nominee), a family decides to become a Crevice Crew; the Crevice Crew selects a situation from the "want" list and makes sure the circumstances of the Nominee are at least a rational, if not perfect, match; the Crevice Crew and the Nominee work out a plan to attain social integration and individual responsibility for the Nominee (household). This plan is reduced to a written contract; the Crevice Crew then sets about facilitating the progress of the Nominee through to execution of the contract (resulting in social integration and individual responsibility). This might be a three to five-year project. It should only last longer if a genuine friendship amongst equals develops out of the original project.

The Crevice Crew is not only responsible for facilitation, encouragement, and moral support. It is also responsible for marshalling the right level of resources. For example, getting friends and neighbours to: host vacations, weekends, sporting events; attend school plays, church programs, organized games in which the Nominee household members are participating; and find information, jobs, clothing, furniture, hobby materials, sports equipment.

The education requirements will be provided for as described in the education chapter. However, the costs of transportation, housing, food, and clothing will still need to be met through the efforts of the Nominee, the Crevice Crew, and the other participants found by the Crevice Crew.

One might assume the Crevice Crew would have to be a family with lots of money, lots of contacts, and lots of free time. However, the key ingredient will be a genuine commitment to facilitating the social integration and individual responsibility of the Nominee. I grew up in a responsible family with low disposable income. Our social activities included: frequent Sunday dinners at an Aunt and Uncle's home where our family provided many of the facilitating functions proposed for the Crevice Crews; regular attendance at the local church, participating in Sunday School, confirmation classes, church picnics, church programs, church administration; regular participation in the community baseball league regular participation in the local farm and community organizations; and social outings including potluck dinners, school Christmas concerts, crokinole and whist tournaments, turkey shoots, community sports days, baseball tournaments. All of these were organized and staged by the local families. There was none of the splash of the Canadian National Exhibition or Calgary Stampede. I never attended a midway until I was 20 years old.

My Mom was co-opted into making costumes out of salvaged materials for our dreams. My Dad was routinely asked to help neighbours with repairing equipment, wiring farmsteads when electricity came to the community, renovating community buildings, supervising threshing crews, and any other activity requested of him. This listing of activities is not meant to put my family on any pedestal, but rather to illustrate social fabric can be woven on a very thin financial budget. Rural settings are different than urban settings. Expectations are perhaps higher, but should they be? Real satisfaction comes with doing well with resources at hand. Some will grow to great heights; some will fail; but the majority will be substantially content with doing well without making the cover of People magazine.

You might ask where governments, service clubs, churches, and community associations can fit into the suggested social order. My suggestions follow: government can get out of the way. Repeal social engineering laws such as minimum wages, young offenders legislation, restrictions on schooling options, worker's compensation, monopolies, tax deductible donations, ad infinitum; non-government organizations can publish Nominee lists, encourage Crevice Crews, gather funds for special projects, organize old-fashioned, low-cost social and sporting activities; big business can encourage employees to become Crevice Crews, publicize success stories in their house rags, lobby governments to get out of the way, and provide appropriate job opportunities; and small business can do the same as big business, except it is uniquely situated to provide meaningful employment for Nominees because the company policy manual probably doesn't exist.

Central to my proposals for individuals wanting help is a written plan that clarifies what the exercise is expected to achieve. Such a plan (contract) might cover the following matters.

Welfare

Background

What happened to cause me to ask for help?
Have I now agreed I will relentlessly pursue a life of responsibility and independence?
Have I now agreed I am primarily responsible for my own life?

Family Support

What is my relationship with my parents? Other relatives?
Has my family given up on me?
Have I given up on my family?
If the family relationships have failed, what can I do to rebuild those relationships?
If I don't want to rebuild, why?

Mate

Do I have a responsible mate?
If yes, how do we integrate our efforts?
If no, what am I going to do about it?
What are my aspirations for long-term relationships with a mate?
How do I find and keep such a mate?

Dependents

Who am I primarily responsible for?
What other financial obligations do I now have; alimony, garnishees, commitments?
Will dependents live with me?
What are their ages?
Who will care for them while I'm working?

Alcohol, Tobacco, Drugs

What habits do I now have?
How am I going stop?
What is the time frame?
Why should anyone help me if I refuse to help myself?
What is the monitoring system?

Shelter

Where am I going to live?
Who's going to pay for the housing?
How long can this arrangement last?
Is the accommodation suitable?
What is my long-term housing goal?

Food

How am I going to get groceries?
Who is going to pay for them?
How will I achieve balanced meals?

Clothing

What kind of clothes do I need?
Where are they going to come from?
Who's going to pay the cost of clothing?
How will I get access to laundry facilities?
What kind of clothes will let me feel comfortable?

Education

What education do I have now?
If inadequate, how do I upgrade?
How do I fit education in my schedule?

Welfare

Who is going to pay for it?
What will I consider success in my education?

Career Choice

What do I want to do to earn a living?
What steps are required to get there?
Who do I want to help me?
How do I measure my progress?

Transportation

How do I get to work?
Who pays the cost?
How do children get to school?
Auto purchase costs?
Auto operating costs?
Auto insurance costs; out of sight due to drinking, speeding, carelessness?

What Is Success?

How will I know I have succeeded?
Financial independence?
Stable relationship with mate?
Children progressing okay?
Adequate food, clothing, shelter?
Feeling of accomplishment?
Own home?
Predictable retirement?

Mentor

What kind of person would make a good personal mentor for me?

How will I find this person?
What do I have to do to live up to the Mentor's expectations?
Am I genuinely willing to try?
What if I fail?
Why should the Mentor take on the task?

Contract Headings

Key person
Mentor
Timeframe
Philosophy
Vision
Mission
Objectives of the key person
Transition steps
Budget management

Chapter 12 Constituencies and Wards

I articulate constituency related suggestions consistent with my philosophy and approach to governance in Canada. There will be flaws. Many will propose improvements. I welcome full discussion with hope we can find solutions which build on individual responsibility.

Under the existing system, there is little evidence governments know the current address of their citizens, or even how many citizens they have. Under my proposals, every individual would have an identification number assigned at birth or at entry to the country on any basis other than a visit. From the identification number administration, the system could maintain last known addresses for every individual.

Because addresses are known, the constituencies for federal, provincial, and municipal jurisdictions would be automatically established by assigning individuals by postal codes in a pattern as near to a contiguous square as possible. The constituencies would be adjusted prior to each election by the total population of the whole jurisdiction, divided by the number of constituencies/wards. This would be a mechanical exercise not affected by partisan considerations, nature of residents, wealth, occupation, age, or anything else. Simple rules of rounding would be in place to get the populations of the constituencies/wards close while honoring postal code designations.

All levels of government would be expected to maintain integrity of the addresses of individuals. Therefore, every contact with police and government bureaucracies would routinely get the identification numbers of individuals and the updated addresses.

Since every individual is required to file an annual return, there is annual opportunity to receive an address for each individual. The Individual Obligations Act includes a penalty for not filing the annual return.

Since the Life Security Plan program is funded by income that would otherwise be remitted as tax, the federal government would have continuous access to the following data in every Life Security Plan: individual's name; individual's identification number; individual's address; and individual's Life Security Plan current balance.

The combination of information sources indicates few could live in Canada without coming into contact with a means of ensuring the individual was authorized to be here. The 10-year census was put in the constitution a century and a half ago when the recordkeeping tools were different. Today the 10-year census is useless. It probably will not identify the illegal residents and is redundant for the law-abiding masses.

Chapter 13 Constitution

I articulate constitution related suggestions consistent with my philosophy and approach to governance in Canada. There will be flaws. Many will propose improvements. I welcome full discussion with hope we can find solutions which build on individual responsibility.

"Power is regarded by all men as the greatest of temporal advantages. The support given to Power, therefore, is an obligation; and, consequently, the protection given by governors to subjects, a positive duty. The subject can only be bound to obedience on the considerations of public good; but the Sovereign, on these considerations, and a thousand others equally binding, is tied to the exact observance of the laws of the constitution under which he holds his power." Catherine Macaulay (Graham) (1731-1791); An Address to the People of England, Scotland, and Ireland, on the Present Important Crisis of Affairs

"Individuals have rights, and there are things no person or group may do to them (without violating their rights). So strong and far-reaching are these rights that they raise the question of what, if anything, the state and its officials may do . . . Our main conclusions about the state are that a minimal state, limited to the narrow functions of protection against force, theft, fraud, enforcement of contracts, and so on, is justified; that any more extensive state will violate persons' rights not to be forced to do certain things, and is unjustified; and that the minimal state is

inspiring as well as right." Robert Nozick (b. 1938); Anarchy, State, and Utopia, p. ix

This chapter invites all Canadians to embark on a scavenger hunt to find a group of treasures Canadians rationally believe to be suitable for their Constitution.

Since many wince at the mention of the Constitution, this hunt will be code-named "Bedrock."

Under the rules of "Bedrock", you can roam the world for treasures. There is no master list to say who wins. At the end of the hunt, all Canadians will be asked to vote on each of the proffered treasures. Each treasure receiving 80% approval of those voting will be accepted as a valid treasure, so long as the affirmative votes represent at least 67% of all the eligible voters in the country.

The valid treasures will be assembled into a polished arrangement and placed as "Bedrock" on which all Canadians can build their futures with confidence and pride.

The hunt will end when all interested Canadians have voted on the proffered treasures. The prize will be world leadership in human governance.

Following are the clauses I believe will capture wide approval. There will be opportunities to identify flaws, improve wording, and debate repercussions. My guidelines include the following: individuals are the key, official discrimination is generally untenable, human nature will prevail, and bold moves are easier to sell than incremental moves.

Constitution

Individual Responsibilities and Rights

100 Canadians believe each mature individual is primarily responsible for maintaining sustenance, freedom, order, and tradition. This Constitution allows individuals to meet their obligations and protects their rights.

"Now it is evident that that form of government is best in which every man, whoever he is, can act best and live happily." Aristotle (384 BC-322 BC); Politics, 1324a

101 So long as any individual has not avoided lawful custody, that individual shall not be deprived of life nor liberty.

102 No law abiding individual shall be forced to act against his/her own mind.

"Liberty is then neither more nor less than the absence of coercion. This is the genuine, original and proper sense of the word Liberty. The idea of it is an idea purely negative. It is not anything that is produced by positive Law. It exists without Law, and not by means of Law." Jeremy Bentham (1748-1832); Bentham Manuscripts, University College London, LXIX, 44

"For . . . what liberty is; there can no other proof be offered but every man's own experience, by reflection on himself, and remembering what he useth in his mind, that is, what he himself meaneth when he saith an action . . . is free. Now he that reflecteth so on himself, cannot but be satisfied . . . that a free agent is he that can do if he will, and forbear if he will; and that liberty is the absence of external impediments. But to those that out of custom speak not what they conceive, but what they heard, and are not able, or will not take the pains to consider what they think when they hear such words, no argument can be sufficient, because experience and matter of fact are not verified by other men's arguments, but by every man's own sense and memory." Thomas Hobbes (1588-1679); Of Liberty and Necessity, English Works, 4, p.275

103 Each citizen is equal before the law and is entitled to equal protection of the law.

Toward Improving Canada

". . . all inequality that has no special utility to justify it is injustice." *Jeremy Bentham (1748-1832); Supply Without Burthen or Escheat Vice Taxation, Jeremy Bentham's Economic Writings, ed. W. Stark, I, p. 329*

104 Except where there is compelling reason to believe that an individual could inflict serious physical harm to those around them, there shall be no discrimination against any citizen of Canada by any government authority.

"The object of this essay is to assert one very simple principle as entitled to govern absolutely the dealings of society with the individual in the way of compulsion and control, whether the means used be physical coercion in the form of legal penalties, or the moral coercion of public opinion. That principle is, that the sole end for which mankind are warranted, individually or collectively, in interfering with the liberty of action of any of their number, is self-protection . . . the only purpose for which power can be rightfully exercised over any member of a civilized community, against his will, is to prevent harm to others. His own good, either physical or moral, is not a sufficient warrant. He cannot rightfully be compelled to do or forbear because it will be better for him to do so, because it will make him happier, because, in the opinion of others, to do so would be wise, or even right . . . The only part of the conduct of any one, for which he is amenable to society, is that which concerns others. In the part which merely concerns himself, his independence is, of right, absolute. Over himself, over his own body and mind, the individual is sovereign." *John Stuart Mill (1806-1873); On Liberty, p. 223*

105 No citizen of Canada shall be banished nor excluded from Canada.

106 Each law abiding citizen of Canada has the right to move freely throughout Canada, to reside anywhere in Canada, participate in the economy anywhere in Canada, and to own property anywhere in Canada.

Constitution

107 Each citizen of Canada has the right to freedom of speech and expression, except where such speech and expression is both libelous and directed at an identifiable individual and/or household.

108 Each citizen of Canada has the right to assemble peaceably without arms.

109 Each citizen of Canada has the right to form associations.

110 No individual or entity shall be forced to comply with terms of a commercial arrangement where the individual or entity has not freely agreed to the arrangement.

111 Each citizen of Canada has the right to profess, practice, and propagate any religion, so long as that citizen complies with all clauses of this Constitution.

112 Each citizen (and entity controlled by Canadian citizens) has the right to own property. Such ownership shall be evidenced by written contract, freely signed. No government authority shall deprive any citizen (or entity controlled by Canadian citizens) of property acquired or developed in accordance with Canadian law, except by way of expropriation at a price that is equal to the higher of fair market value at the time of acquisition by the current owner and the price arising from the following formula:

FMV x Years x 2, where:

"FMV" equals the highest fair market value of the target property in the time period from notice of expropriation to 30 days prior to full payment.

"Years" equals the number of years that the target property was continuously held by the extended family of the present owner [or legal entity(ies) controlled by such extended family]. Part years shall be calculated on the basis of days in the part year.

"If one force is to compel respect from another force, each must be independent of the other. They must be two distinct forces, not one. If, therefore, the citizen is to count for anything in the State, personal freedom is not enough. His individuality, like that of the State, must be founded on something material over

which he must have sovereign possession, just as the State has sovereign possession over public property. Private property provides this foundation." Pierre-Joseph Proudhon (1809-1865); The Theory of Property, p. 135

113 Each citizen of Canada of any age shall be eligible to vote in the federal, provincial, and municipal jurisdiction of primary residence, provided only that such individual has (once in a lifetime) successfully completed a written examination demonstrating a rudimentary knowledge of the Canadian Constitution, federal issues of the day, provincial issues of the day, municipal issues of the day, and individuals prominently involved in the community. A young child citizen may demonstrate the contemplated rudimentary knowledge and, therefore, be eligible to vote in any jurisdiction of primary residence.

114 No group of governments in Canada shall charge one individual in Canada more tax in total than that group of governments charges the majority of individuals in the relevant jurisdictions in any calendar year.

115 Where any government in Canada restricts the actions of any citizen, such restrictions shall be strictly limited to situations where there is compelling reason to believe the citizen could inflict serious physical harm to individuals around him/her. Examples of acceptable restrictions include minimum age limits for driving vehicles and operating firearms, and detention of suspected and convicted criminals. Examples of unacceptable restrictions include age restrictions on voting, drinking alcoholic beverages, smoking, consensual sexual activity, curfews, mandatory retirement, signing of contracts, ownership of property, and consensual employment.

116 Where any individual is found guilty of an indictable offence and subsequently avoids the highest level of custody, such avoidance of custody removes protection of life from that individual's Constitutional rights.

117 Each individual shall be considered innocent until proven guilty. In order to protect the reputation of individuals and other entities prior to evidence of culpability, there shall be a general prohibition on publication of criminal charges and civil claims until such time as a Court has ruled the individual guilty in a criminal matter or an arbitration panel has ruled the party liable in a civil matter.

"Publicity is the very soul of justice. It is the keenest spur to exertion, and the surest of all guards against improbity. It keeps the judge himself, while trying, under trial. Under the auspices of publicity, the cause in the court of law, and the appeal to the court of public opinion, are going on at the same time . . . . It is through publicity alone that justice becomes the mother of security." Jeremy Bentham (1748-1832); Draught of a Code for the Organization of the Judicial Establishment in France, Works, IV, p .316

118 Each resident of Canada shall report once each calendar year to no more than three levels of government. Such report shall designate the tax to be paid by the individual and shall indicate the programs approved by that resident. Where the resident is not capable of reporting, such reports and taxes shall be filed by a parent or guardian.

119 Each elected individual who votes in the affirmative for a law that is passed into law and is subsequently determined by the Supreme Court of Canada to violate the Constitution shall be immediately barred for life from holding any elected position in any government in Canada and shall be barred for life from employment by any government authority in Canada.

120 Every individual in Canada is entitled to domestic protection by a system of police, courts, and penalties.

121 No government in Canada shall tax, discriminate against, nor restrict the flow of citizens, goods, services, vehicles, information, intellectual property, or any other thing within Canada.

Justice

201 Canada's judiciary shall be comprised of four levels as follows: a Supreme Court of Canada; a Provincial Court for each province; a Municipal Court for each municipality; and an Arbitration process.

202 All criminal cases shall be initially tried at the Municipal Court of the municipality in which the crime was committed, with appeal processes to the Provincial and Supreme Courts.

203 All civil cases shall be initially arbitrated, with appeal processes to Municipal, Provincial, and Supreme Courts.

204 Supreme Court judges shall be: citizens of Canada; nominated by a province; approved by a majority of provinces approved by the House of Commons; approved by the Senate; and ratified by the Governor-General.

205 Provincial Court judges shall be: citizens of Canada; nominated by a municipality approved by a majority of municipalities in the relevant province; approved by the Legislature; ratified by the Governor-General; and never have been admitted into the legal profession in any jurisdiction in the world.

206 Municipal Court judges shall be: citizens of Canada; nominated by a nominating committee of twenty-five individuals who substantially reflect the mix of the residents in the municipality; approved by the municipal council; and ratified by the Governor-General.

207 Arbiters shall be: citizens of Canada; qualified by meeting the terms and conditions of the Chartered Arbiters of Canada professional body; never have been admitted into the legal profession in any jurisdiction in the world; and assigned to individual cases by random selection from the list of available arbiters in the extended community comprising the provincial constituencies adjacent to the provincial constituency in which the respondent resides (in the case of an non-individual, the address of the entity).

208 Judges shall be appointed for eight-year terms and shall not be subjected to, nor participate in, communication concerning any judicial matter by any elected member of any government during the Judge's term.

209 Arbiters shall be subject to the ethics of the Chartered Arbiters of Canada professional code of conduct.

Education

301 Every citizen shall have the right to attend educational institutions for sixty modules of education; where each module shall cover three months and include at least sixty days of instruction. Such sixty days shall comprise at least three hundred hours of formal instruction. This clause is subject to the following: no individual shall be entitled to the next module of publicly-funded instruction until the latest module attempted has been successfully completed; while the reasonable cost of materials and premises are to be publicly-funded, there shall be no obligation for any government to provide transportation, food, or clothing to students.

Expenditure Limits

401 So long as no war is currently declared in Canada, the federal government shall not spend more in any calendar year than it collects in revenue.

402 No provincial nor municipal government shall spend more in any calendar year than it collects in revenue.

403 Expenditures and revenues shall be recorded on the basis of generally accepted accounting principles in Canada.

Citizenship

501 Individuals who are not citizens of Canada shall be allowed to enter as immigrants on a strict and scrupulous "first requested, first allowed" basis with the following absolute restrictions: no individual shall be allowed to enter Canada as an immigrant if that individual carries a communicable disease; no individual shall be allowed to enter Canada as an immigrant if that individual has a criminal record involving incarceration of more than two years or more than one criminal offence; no individual shall be allowed to enter Canada as an immigrant unless the federal government has not filled the federal immigration quota as published on January 1 of the year of authorization to enter; no individual shall be allowed to enter Canada as an immigrant unless that individual takes up residence in a municipality that has not yet filled its immigration quota as published on January 1 of the year of authorization to enter; no individual shall be allowed to enter Canada as an immigrant unless that individual demonstrates that the individual has established a Life Security Plan funded to the level required by the Life Security Index for the age of the individual; any individual in Canada who is not a citizen shall be deported without compensation upon conviction of an indictable offence. In this case, the net funds in the individual's Life Security Plan shall be released in total to the individual; prior to the granting of citizenship, an immigrant must meet the following requirements: be proficient in reading, writing, and speaking the dominant language in the province of primary residence; ensure the Life Security Plan contains the funds required by the Life Security Index for the age of the individual; and demonstrate the rudimentary knowledge required of every individual before voting in Canada.

502 Children born in Canada to mothers who are not citizens shall not be citizens of Canada until: the mother of the child born in Canada becomes a citizen of Canada and is resident in Canada;

and the Life Security Plans of both the mother and the child contain the funds required by the Life Security Index for the ages of the individuals involved.

503 Individuals born outside of Canada to a mother that is a Canadian citizen shall be granted citizenship when: the mother and the relevant dependent child become resident in Canada and the Life Security Plans of the mother and relevant dependent child contain the funds required by the Life Security Index for the ages of the individuals involved.

504 Neither the biological nor adoptive father of a child has any bearing on the Canadian citizenship status of the child.

Sovereignty

601 Any Canadian lands owned by any government may be sold to other Canadian governments, legal non-government entities, or individuals at the discretion of the owner.

602 There shall be no surrender nor transfer, either wholly or in part, of the sovereignty of Canada as an independent nation.

603 There shall be no surrender nor transfer, either wholly or in part, of the lands and waters presently designated as Canadian lands and waters.

Governor-General

701 There shall be a Governor-General of Canada who shall be the Head of State and shall exercise and perform such powers and functions as are conferred on the Governor-General by this Constitution.

702 The Governor-General shall be elected by the citizens of Canada in a general election held every four years. Such general election to be held on the third Monday in October, commencing with October 19, 2020.

703 Any candidate for Governor-General shall be a Canadian citizen and shall have been active in independent

enterprise for at least the twenty-five years preceding first election as Governor-General. Such independent enterprise shall have had no significant revenues from any government authority in Canada. Furthermore, the Governor-General shall not have been admitted to the legal profession anywhere in the world. This clause is specifically provided to ensure that proposed actions by government coming before the Governor-General will be reviewed by a competent individual who has not been steeped in government bureaucracy and/or legal doctrine.

704 No Governor-General shall serve more than eight years.

705 Vacancy in the position of Governor-General shall be filled by a general election coincident with the next scheduled federal election. Temporary vacancies shall be filled by appointment of an individual meeting the criteria and appointed after the written approval of at least two-thirds of the provincial Premiers.

706 The Governor-General shall sign into law such proposed federal law that comes before the Governor-General provided that; the proposed law complies with this Constitution, a majority of the members of the Senate has passed the law, a majority of the members of the House of Commons has passed the law, and a majority of the residents of the country have indicated approval of the emerging program in twelve consecutive months.

707 Where the Governor-General believes the proposed law is not appropriate as proposed, the Governor-General shall, within thirty days of receiving the proposed law for signature, table in the House of Commons such written explanation as he/she deems appropriate. The House of Commons shall reconsider the proposed law in light of the Governor-General's written explanations and shall vote again on the proposed law. If the proposed law remains unchanged, the Governor-General shall sign it forthwith. If there is any change, the proposed law shall be subjected to the same scrutiny as any other proposed law.

708 The Supreme Court of Canada shall rule on any point of law put to it by the Governor-General concerning any law

currently in force in Canada. Such ruling shall be made within 90 days of original, written request.

709 Remuneration of the Governor-General shall be $44,000 per month, plus/minus consumer price index since 2014, to cover all remuneration, including housing, travel, security, and all other expenses. No amount beyond the $44,000 per month, plus/minus consumer price index since 2015, shall be paid by any government authority to the Governor-General.

Jurisdictions

Federal

801 Canada shall maintain a federal government with responsibility for the following: Parliament, Justice, Defense, Treasury Board, Immigration, Air and Water, Communicable Disease Control, and Federal Revenue.

802 Where the Constitution does not grant powers to a specific level of government, such powers shall be subject to the mandate of a majority of the voters in a jurisdiction. If more than 50% of the country's population, and more that 50% of eight provinces' populations, supports a discretionary program, it shall be a federal program.

Parliament

803 There shall be a Senate of Canada which shall provide sober second thought to any proposed law passed by the House of Commons.

804 There shall be three democratically-elected Senators from each province.

805 Elections to the Senate shall be held every four years on the third Monday in October, commencing with October 19, 2020.

806 No proposed law shall pass the Senate unless more than half of all elected Senators vote for the proposed law.

Toward Improving Canada

807 Vacancies in the Senate shall be filled at the next scheduled federal election. Temporary vacancies shall be filled by an individual appointed after the written approval of two-thirds of the Municipal Mayors/Reeves in the province having the vacancy.

808 Remuneration of Senators shall be $96,000 per annum, plus/minus consumer price index from 2015. Such amount is a flat contract of $8,000 per month, plus/minus consumer price index from 2015. The Senate shall convene for a period up to seven days per quarter of a year. The federal government shall provide reasonable accommodation and travel services for the Senators during the four sessions per year. No other amounts, including pensions, shall be paid by any government authority to any current or past Senator.

809 No Senator shall serve more than eight years.

810 There shall be a House of Commons which shall debate laws and approve laws to be forwarded to the Senate for sober second thought.

811 There shall be one hundred and thirty democratically-elected Members of Parliament from across Canada.

812 Constituencies shall be blocks as nearly rectangular as possible and made up of whole postal codes (first three characters) representing 1/130 of the number of residents in the country as of December 31 of the year prior to the election.

813 Elections to the House of Commons shall be held every four years on the third Monday in October, commencing with October 19, 2020.

814 No proposed law shall pass the House of Commons unless more than half of all elected Members of Parliament vote for the proposed law.

815 Vacancies in the House of Commons shall be filled at by-elections scheduled no later than one hundred and eighty days subsequent to definitive vacancy.

816 Remuneration of Members of Parliament shall be $96,000 per annum, plus/minus consumer price index from 2015.

Such amount is a flat contract amount of $8,000 per month, plus/minus consumer price index from 2015. Parliament shall convene for a period up to 14 days per quarter of a year. The federal government shall provide reasonable accommodation and travel costs for the Members of Parliament during the four sessions per year. No other amounts, including pensions, shall be paid by any government authority to any current or past Member of Parliament.

817 The elected Members of Parliament shall democratically elect the Prime Minister from the ranks of the elected Members of Parliament.

818 The Prime Minister shall receive an additional $960,000, plus/minus consumer price index from 2015 to cover all remuneration, including housing, staff, travel, security, and all other expenses. Such amount, including basic remuneration, is a flat $88,000 per month, plus/minus consumer price index. No amount beyond the $88,000 per month, plus/minus consumer price index from 2015 shall be reimbursed by any government authority to the Prime Minister.

Provincial

819 Canada shall be divided into 13 provinces.

820 Each province shall, subject to provisions in this Constitution and majority approval of the residents, have jurisdiction over: provincial courts; the environment, except air and water; natural resources; and education.

821 There shall be a Legislature in each province which shall debate and approve laws to be forwarded to the Governor-General for ratification.

822 There shall be no more than twenty-five members of each provincial Legislature democratically-elected from no more than twenty-five constituencies in the province. Each constituency in the province shall have substantially equal numbers of eligible voters.

823 Elections to the provincial Legislatures shall be held every four years on the third Monday in October, commencing with October 19, 2020.

824 No proposed law shall pass the Legislature unless more than half of all elected Members of the Legislature vote for the proposed law.

825 Vacancies in the provincial Legislatures shall be filled at by-elections scheduled no later than one hundred and eighty days subsequent to definitive vacancy.

826 Constituencies shall be blocks as nearly rectangular as possible and made up of whole postal codes (first three characters) representing substantially equal numbers of residents in the province as of December 31 of the year prior to the election.

827 Where the Constitution does not grant powers to a specific level of government, such powers shall be subject to the mandate of a majority of the voters in a jurisdiction. If more than 50% of a province's population supports a discretionary program that is not a federal discretionary program, it shall be the province's program.

Municipal

828 Each province shall be divided into municipalities.

829 Each municipality shall, subject to provisions in this Constitution, appropriate provincial laws, and majority approval of the residents, have jurisdiction over: municipal courts; police; roads; and zoning.

830 There shall be a Municipal Council in each municipality which shall debate and approve laws.

831 There shall be a minimum of five Councillors and a maximum of twenty-five Councillors democratically-elected from the equivalent number of wards having substantially equal numbers of eligible voters. Wards shall be blocks as nearly rectangular as possible and made up of whole postal codes (first

three characters) representing (one/divided by the number of Councillors) times the number of eligible voters in the municipality as of December 31 of the year prior to the election.

832 Elections to the Municipal Councils shall be held every four years on the third Monday in October, commencing with October 19, 2020.

833 No proposed law shall pass the Municipal Council unless more than half of all elected Councillors vote for the proposed law.

834 Vacancies in the Municipal Councils shall be filled in by-elections scheduled no later than one hundred and eighty days subsequent to definitive vacancy.

835 Where the Constitution does not clearly grant powers to a specific level of government, such powers shall be subject to the mandate of a majority of the voters in a jurisdiction. If more than 50% of a municipality's population supports a discretionary program that is not a federal nor a provincial discretionary program, it shall be the municipality's program.

Defeats of Bills

836 No government shall be forced to resign because of the defeat of any bill.

Election of Prime Minister, Premier, Mayor

837 Any democratically-elected government may select a new chairperson (Prime Minister, Premier, Mayor) by a simple majority of all elected members in that government. Ratification or replacement of the chairperson shall occur within thirty days of written petition signed by at least twenty percent of all elected members in the relevant body. Any elected member of the body may stand for election as chairperson at any vote regarding the selection or ratification of the chairperson.

838 Any elected individual in any government in Canada is subject to recall by constituents. Such recall shall be subject to the following rules: At least 5% of the eligible voters in the jurisdiction must sign a petition requesting recall. Upon receipt of a valid petition for recall, the Governor-General shall convene a panel of three arbiters: One named by the elected individual targeted for recall. One named by the petitioners at the time the petition was signed. One mutually agreed to by the above two arbiters. Failing agreement within fifteen days, a third arbiter shall be appointed by the Provincial Court in the home province of the member targeted for recall. The third arbiter shall chair the panel. Such panel of arbiters shall hear evidence and provide a written ruling approved by at least two arbiters within sixty days of the filing of the petition. Such ruling shall be binding. The panel shall not be bound by formal rules of evidence, but shall be guided by fundamental fairness. No recall petition shall be acted upon if submitted within two years of the submission of a prior recall petition concerning the same elected individual.

Insurrection

900 Where the federal government declares an insurrection, notwithstanding anything in this Constitution, the federal government may make laws which it believes to be required by reason of the insurrection. Such laws must be ratified by a simple majority in a special national referendum within one hundred and twenty days of passing into law. Such laws shall be further subject to ratification every two years. Every second such ratification process shall coincide with the national election.

War

1000 Where the federal government declares war, notwithstanding anything in this Constitution, the federal government may make laws which it believes to be required by reason of the war. Such laws must be ratified by a simple majority in a special national referendum within one hundred and twenty days of passing into law. Such laws shall be further subject to ratification every two years. Every second such ratification process shall coincide with the national election.

Name

1100 The name of the country shall be "Canada".

Supremacy

1200 This Constitution shall be supreme in Canada. No law shall be valid which violates this Constitution.

Constitutional Amendments

1300 This Constitution shall not be amended except by the affirmative vote of 80% of those citizens of Canada voting on such amendment and provided that the affirmative votes cast represent at least 67% of the entire number of eligible voters.

1301 Any amendments shall be voted upon on a clause-by-clause basis with no opportunity to force the voters to consider any omnibus amendment

Further the Journey

This book was drafted in the early 2000s. The original impetus was an invitation by the CA Magazine for Chartered Accountants to suggest ways to improve our government. I published my suggestions on the internet as a free document but I didn't merchandise my ideas except for casual mention as opportunities arose. Subsequent to publishing my novel, Tunnel Vision, I decided to polish Toward Improving Canada for wider exposure. This is the result.

I'm writing an updated version of Toward Improving Canada entitled Village Café A Buffet of Ideas. Most of the concepts are parallel but the narrative is less tied to Canada and the examples have been updated to reflect: refined ideas, changes in the economy, and deeper penetration of social media. Watch for Village Café late in 2015. If both books are available to you; choose Village Café.

Tunnel Vision is a novel, set in northern Canada, which builds on my philosophy. You're invited to read the novel and help build better villages. The first sixteen chapters of Tunnel Vision are reproduced as the last part of this book.

If you know someone who's interested in good answers, please encourage them to read Tunnel Vision and add perspectives to the issues.

Connect with me online:

My blog: http://www.VillageSource.net

Facebook: http://www.facebook.com/VillageSourceDotNet

Twitter: http://www.twitter.com/@DaveAmonson

I encourage you to follow me on Facebook and Twitter. You can follow by clicking on the appropriate boxes on my website. Each of my blogs provides an opportunity to comment on the particular blog. This is effective because the comments are sorted with the original blog. If you wish to contact me privately, my email is (my nickname and last name with no spaces)@VillageSource.net

About the Author

Dave Amonson grew up on a small mixed farm in northeastern British Columbia. He is the middle of five children born to Jennie and Percy Amonson. After high school, Dave worked in geophysical exploration for five years before attending the University of Calgary. He earned a B. Comm. Accounting major with distinction and articled with Arthur Andersen & Co. He co-founded ALW Partners LLP, Chartered Accountants in 1979 and continues as a partner in that firm.

Always interested in supporting his communities, Dave has served on multiple committees for accounting, community, and political organizations. In 2001, Dave was honored by his peers with a Fellow Chartered Accountant designation.

In 2015, he published his first novel, Tunnel Vision. He's currently working on revisions to the ideas in Towards Improving Canada by extending applicability to any place on earth. The new version is called Village Café, a buffet of ideas. Watch for it in the fall of 2015.

Dave lives with his wife Bernadette in Cochrane, Alberta. His children and grandchildren live in Calgary

Other Dimensions

Belief Consensus Community (Village) Constitution Democracy Education Engagement Environment Fairness Family First Nations Good Persons Harvest Justice Life Security Myth Power Property Rights Public Interest Rational Laws Reason Respect Ribbons & Jewels Soul Taker-Maker Taxation Trust Villager Philosophy

All of these topics can be explored on
www.VillageSource.net

Contact the Author

My preferred communication, with you, is through the comment area following each blog on
www.VillageSource.net
This allows me to pay attention to one flow of communications without developing substantial administrative infrastructure.

See the information under the preceding caption further the journey.Tunnel Vision, a Novel by Dave Amonson

Tunnel Vision

A Novel by Dave Amonson

Following are the first sixteen chapters of my only novel. If you appreciate the ideas in Village Cafe; I think you'll enjoy, Tunnel Vision

Chapter 1

Two captains in dress whites emerge into the sunshine. Youths from every nation follow. The nearest ocean is two thousand kilometers away.

Twelve years earlier, drizzle fell on the remnants of a graveside service. Mourners moved toward their cars. A father and both daughters, hand in hand, lingered by the grave.

After the funeral lunch, as the sky lightened, Elaine asked Brett, "Will you walk with me in Bowness Park?"

"Sure, let's go by the house and change clothes on our way."

The sunlight reflected off the water in a pond. A glint of light caught Brett's attention.

Could a tiny spot of light change the trajectory of a life?

Elaine sensed his mood. "What're you thinking?"

He pointed to the far bank. "Do you see that spot of light?"

Elaine leaned closer to him. "Yes, I see it."

"I wonder whether I might provide a speck of light to deflect a person's path toward a better life."

"You do that all the time."

"Marjie occupied our circle for twenty-eight years. She missed the light; she's dead."

She turned to him. "Are you responsible for everyone?"

"No, but there're lots of Marjies in this world. Do you think we could help a bunch of them?"

"We're near retirement. I have visions of times with the children and grandchildren, quiet times in the garden, sorties to visit friends and relatives, a peaceful golden age. Are you going to shatter my dream?"

Chapter 2

Beth approached Brett's café table. "Hi, old friend, good to see you."

"Hi, Beth, it's been awhile. How're you doing?"

"Fine. I'm busy and enjoying life's little challenges."

"Remember when we worked through the weekend until one-thirty Monday morning, so we could accommodate the customer's final inspection on time?"

"Do you remember my words to you? Next time, let me manage the job. Mac was angry because I missed his parents' anniversary party. He went alone."

"Was that the last straw for Mac?"

She shrugged. "No, he viewed marriage as a joint endeavour but I ran it. He ran."

"I'm sorry I caused one more rift. Your ability to manage projects was a lifesaver but we should've accommodated our families more. Still, Mac wasn't the only guy in town."

"No, but I prefer TV. No drama when I turn it off."

He smiled. "You must have been born after the Romantic Period."

"And you're the perfect marriage partner?"

"No, not perfect. That's why I invited you to lunch. I've got an idea; Elaine doesn't like it. I want to run it by you."

"I'm supposed to help you sell an idea that Elaine doesn't like. This should improve things."

He sipped his coffee. "It's a tunnel from the mouth of the St. Lawrence to Whitehorse; it'll provide material for a multipurpose transportation-utility corridor across the northern expanse of Canada with townhouses along each side. I want to use labour plucked from youth that choose not to integrate in conventional settings. The project will be a viable alternative to welfare."

Beth ordered coffee and looked at Brett. "I spent school breaks at my uncle's cattle ranch. One spring, Uncle noticed a cow in trouble. As we chased her toward the corral, she charged me. I ducked behind a tree. Uncle got his horse between me and the cow. She was delirious from her dead calf rotting inside her. The vet wasn't available for several hours, so Uncle shot the cow, ending her misery. As you described your idea, I considered whether a hallucinating geezer could be shot. Probably not. Tell me about feeding young blood to mosquitoes and draining Lake Athabasca."

"I want to convince my family I can make this project work. Elaine wants to relax, share time with the children and grandchildren, travel, and socialize. I'll go crazy. I hope you'll help me consider the possibility that I could make this happen. Outside of my family, you're my best friend."

"They'll shut this joint's lights off before I recite all that's wrong with your idea. There're hundreds of interest groups lined up to thwart any project. The Indian situation has been screwed up for a 150 years. The national and provincial parks, Indian reservations, wetlands where a trumpeting swan lands every twenty years, half a dozen provincial and territorial governments, and thousands of individuals will resist any idea, even if it's a good one. It takes money to build a tool shed—try building two townhouses 4,400 kilometers long. A professor tried to teach me negative numbers. I never noticed a need for the concept. Now, I see negative numbers could illustrate the probability you could make this work."

"So you think it might not work?"

She waved her hand. "Oh, I think it'll be as easy as getting an ice cream at the dairy bar. Don't you see it's impossible?"

"Did the Wrights learn how to fly? Did Bell get a phone to work? Did Watt figure out how to improve steam engines? You might be talking to the next great innovator."

"I might be, but I like my odds better than yours."

"Will you come to the grand opening when my project is finished?"

"Of course, my TV will escort me."

Chapter 3

Monday evening, Elaine and Brett ate dinner at home.

Brett raised his glass of water. "I want to lead a change in our social welfare system. What evening could we set aside to talk it through?"

She wiggled her fork. "Don't you listen? I don't want to be involved in obligations. I want us to slow down in retirement."

"I know, but I also know that our serenity must consider our individual interests, and I know I won't be happy line dancing on Tuesday and playing Bingo on Thursday."

"And, if you're not happy, I'm not happy. Is that it?"

"It's not a threat, Elaine. I hope to have a purpose most days, and I don't see satisfaction in idleness."

"Let's have our discussion now and get it over with."

"No, I hope we'll come to some consensus rather than pick at each other forever."

"How will I prepare? I long for a slower pace," Elaine said. "Now, when it's within sight, you go off on some ridiculous tangent."

"I have a suggestion." He put down his fork to indicate his seriousness. "Let's each make a list of the main things we plan for ourselves for the rest of our lives: where we want to live, how much we want to travel, how often we want to visit the grandkids, how much yard work we want to do, where we want to winter, what kinds of hobbies we want, etcetera. We each make our own lists and then we integrate our lists so that each of us gets forty-eight percent of what we want and leave the last four percent for Murphy."

She glanced at him. "Who's Murphy?"

"Murphy's Law, where anything that can go wrong, will go wrong, but we'll plan this so well that nothing will go wrong, right?"

"Wednesday night. You make dinner. I'll sit at the counter, with a glass of wine, and describe my vision and list of wants. I'll clean up the dishes while you tell me your vision and list of wants beyond sex every twenty minutes."

Brett grinned, gave her a thumb up, and rose to pick up the dishes.

Elaine loaded the dishwasher. "What do you plan to do tonight?"

"You've suggested the first forty minutes, then I expect to sleep 'til breakfast."

Chapter 4

Wednesday, Brett brought in the groceries.
Elaine's greeting was abrupt. "Hi."
This'll be piece of cake.

Brett set the bags on the counter. "I bought five minute rice because I didn't want you to have too much time to present your list of hopes and wants."

"And I chilled a bottle of Barolo because I like red wine a tad chilled. It should pair nicely with my shoulder."

He grinned. "Come here, babe. Give me a kiss and let's make this a great evening."

Brett placed two candles on the counter and lit them.

Elaine joined him in the kitchen. "This is a fight to the death. These must be memorial candles?"

"No, the flames will reflect in your eyes until we have a plan that will cause a real spark for the rest of our lives."

"Perhaps you can bottle your crap and sell it door-to-door. It'll give you a reason to get up in the morning. You can call it Bretth Mint, a special blend of dreams and drivel that will dampen every hope and fuel every disagreement. It should sell well."

He faced her. "Forty-seven years ago, I met a spunky little lady who saw potential in me. She has persevered, so far, and I hope she doesn't give up in my remaining thirty years."

Brett began to prepare a meal of wild salmon and stuffed peppers. "So what's on your list?"

"I want you to love me all the time."

"That's easy; I do love you all the time. More than you know."

"Yes, but I want you to demonstrate that love all the time."

"I've worked on that since I met you. You multi-task and thrive on it. I focus and thrive on it. I'll demonstrate my love when I'm focused on it but that won't be often enough to meet your expectations."

"I hope you'll have more time in retirement and you'll have more time for me."

"I'll be around more, but it'll provide more opportunities for you to notice I don't focus enough on demonstrating my love for you. We're a great match. We have similar values. We've raised great kids—they have fine mates and one child. We've not burdened family or society. Why can't we continue to support people and causes we believe in, love each other, and demonstrate our love in ways that match our psyches?"

"You see, the list is hopeless because you never change."

"Is it just me? Do you change? Can we try to find common ground so we can do things that allow each of us to grow and feel fulfilled?"

"I want to live in Calgary. I don't want a home in Phoenix or Timbuktu. I want to be near the kids and grandkids and go to their sports and recitals. I want to continue family dinners on Sunday. I want to have the family together on special occasions."

"I want that, too. We agree one hundred percent."

"How will you do it from your hovel near the Arctic Circle?"

"Perhaps you misunderstood when I said I'd like to lead the initiative, not be the person on site."

"I know, Brett, but there'll be meetings in Ottawa, New York, Vancouver, Whitehorse, Sept Isles, and a trillion other places." She waved her hand in the air in exasperation.

"Have we agreed that Calgary will be our home forever?"

"Yes."

"Do you expect me to be home Friday through Sunday on a regular basis?"

"Yes."

"Does your list allow me some time on Monday through Thursday?"

"Yes, but I don't want you away most of the time."

"That's fair. However, I expect to ask people to commit resources to the project and I'll visit them on occasion. You're welcome to travel with me."

"Yeah, I look forward to hours in the lobby of a hotel in Iqaluit while you schmooze with some government rep."

"Would it help if I find an office within a ten minute walk from here? I can come home for lunch. I'll schedule work and travel for Monday through Thursday. I'll integrate other commitments with you."

"What about the grandchildren's activities? Will you show up to support them?"

"Yes, but probably not as often as you prefer."

She looked at him, a stern expression on her face. "Are you serious about a tunnel clear across Canada?"

"Yes."

"Will it work? When I hear you talk with friends, they laugh and challenge your sanity. What happens when you ask people like that for money and help?"

"Do you remember when we started the construction company? Few people gave us much chance of success. We built the business, we succeeded, and we secured our retirement; why can't we use our skills and contacts to help a bunch of people find their way?"

"Who's we, big boy?"

"I thought you promised to support me, in every little whim that I dreamed up, as long as we both shall live. Will you keep your vows?"

"Only as long as we both shall live; how long will this project consume our lives?"

"About twelve years. Maybe we'll go 'til we drop."

"I can picture you, steadied by your walker, on a rock outcropping in the Yukon. You explain life to some thug from the rough part of Vancouver. He has tattoos all over and seven piercings. You explain to him how you can make him into a young Brett. This has to work out well, don't you think?"

"He might push me off the cliff. I'll die trying to help someone or...he might buy into my approach and become a producer in society, a leader amongst his peers. Either way, I'll have tried."

"I don't want to face life without you."

"It might not be so bad; there're a half million guys waiting for you to emerge from the mist and anoint him as your chosen one. He'll appreciate his libido stored in the deep freeze to be defrosted whenever you put tenderloin on the menu. He'll remember, maybe even care, what dress you wore to the company Christmas party three years ago. He'll come equipped with an early warning system that'll allow him to know how to respond to whatever text, tone, and tenor that bubbles to the surface from the brew that represents your real and imagined life experiences."

She burst into laughter. "Is it that bad?"

"No, but I don't need a higher dose."

"Is supper cooked yet?"

"You're not allowed to change the subject."

"I'm not, I'm multi-tasking."

Brett arranged a garnish of sliced apples, bananas, and grapes, then dished out fish and rice-stuffed peppers, refreshed the wine glasses, and offered his glass. "I love you."

"I love you, too. The salmon is dry."

"On the seventh day, God assembled a woman. She turned out to be complicated. By the time she laughed, the salmon was dry."

Elaine cleaned up the dishes. "It's your turn."

"My list is identical to yours except we differ on the path we'll follow to achieve our continued happiness. You expect me to be more intuitive about situations. When I fail to meet your expectations, you react and widen the chasm. I step back and widen the chasm. We narrow our differences. Each of us can continue to strive to do better, but I'm certain that more opportunities for disconnects will be part of the problem, not the solution."

She held out her hand. "Your stupid tunnel has led to our best discussion in a long time. Come with me; the chill has come off the wine."

Chapter 5

Jeremy, Jacquie, and Simone arrived on Sunday evening. Brett took the bassinette from Jeremy and welcomed little Simone. "Where's King?"

Jacquie took off her jacket. "He threw up this afternoon so we didn't want him to cause a mess in your home or the car."

Erika arrived; Brett took her jacket.

As they gathered around the kitchen counter, the doorbell rang. Sherry stepped in. "Sorry we're late."

With everyone seated around the table, Elaine said, "We have an announcement. Are you ready for a new episode in the Larson world?"

Jeremy looked at her. "Mom, is this charades? Is it good or bad?"

Elaine shrugged. "Ask your father."

Jeremy turned to Brett.

"Elaine and I attended Marjie's funeral some weeks back," Brett began. "I thought about the waste that's caused by young folks losing their way. I want to develop an alternative to social welfare that'll save more troubled youngsters."

Erika asked, "What's this alternative?"

"I want to attract thousands of struggling young people to dig a large tunnel from the St. Lawrence River to the Pacific Ocean and create enough tailings from the tunnel to build a surface transportation-utility corridor across northern Canada that will contain a highway, freight railroad, high speed train, pipelines, townhouses, bicycle paths, and pedestrian walkways."

"Why the tunnel?" Sam asked.

"Two reasons," Brett said. "One, I want to use the tailings to build the raised infrastructure on the surface without damage to the terrain beyond the right of way, and two, I have a secret reason for the tunnel."

Jeremy looked up from his plate. "You intend to dig a tunnel across Canada without full justification. Who's gullible enough to listen?"

"I envision a village, every kilometer along the route, of about 150 individuals who have chosen to develop on this project as an alternative to conventional schools, work experience, and relationship building. These individuals will have decided something has to change to make them happy."

Erika said, "Dad, you describe anarchists. You can't put them all in one place and expect it to work more than three days."

Brett turned to her. "Do you think they are anarchists or are they similar to each of us but less inclined to accept rules that they see as invalid?"

"Mom, this is mad," Erika said, turning to her mother. "Why have you agreed?"

Elaine smiled. "I've talked it through. He wants to try. Haven't we all benefitted from his vision and tenacity? Don't we support each other's dreams?"

Erika said, "You wanted more free time. This sounds like a big job for the old one. Are you sure about this?"

"I'm not sure it will work, but I'm sure we'll try to make it work and I'm hopeful that our kids will support it," Elaine said.

Jacquie smiled and looked at Sherry. "This conversation wouldn't happen between my parents and me. The chemistry is one of Jeremy's attractions. But I see where my life might take some wild turns. I haven't been trained to soar to uncharted heights."

"Or scary depths," Erika added.

"Sam appreciates the latitude he was granted," Sherry said. "My parents support us but they don't exhibit the pioneer instincts visible here tonight."

Jeremy sat up. "Will we let Dad go off on a wild adventure and not talk a little sense into him?"

Elaine refilled Jeremy's glass. "Did we care for you as a baby, did we buy you skates and put you into a hockey league, did we help you learn to read and write and communicate, did we leave you room to choose your own path, did we make room for you to find your mate?" she asked. "Did we do all this because you are more special than your father? I think we did it because it was the right thing to do. Now, your father wants to pursue his mission. Is it too much to ask that we'll support him?"

Erika rose, walked around to her mother, and hugged her. "I love you, Mom."

Elaine anticipated a focused discussion so she put food out after the discussion moderated. Through the meal, the family talked of the opportunities and challenges apparent in Brett's proposal.

After dessert and coffee, Brett said, "I'll try to develop a project that'll be meaningful to each of you while I support family activities. Thanks for your support."

Jeremy shook his dad's hand. "You're lucky you found Mom."

Brett gave him a thumb up. "I know; I hope I'll live up to her faith in me."

Chapter 6

The Larsons gathered at the family home. The guys watched the football game between the Calgary Stampeders and the Montréal Alouettes. The gals made Christmas cards.

The Alouettes scored three touchdowns and a field goal before the Stamps realized the game had started.

Bored and disappointed in the game, Sam asked Brett, "How can 4,400 sponsors be attracted to commit ten million dollars per year for ten years? Didn't you say that the tunnel might cost $100,000 dollars per linear meter?"

Brett lowered the volume on the TV. "And will they see value in the investment?"

Jeremy watched the kick return and surfaced. "There are ways to capture attention, fewer ways to maintain attention, and even fewer ways to sustain it over ten years. It's like a marriage: attraction, passion, trust, respect, and commitment."

Sam feigned shock. "Well, meet my brother, the philosopher."

Brett pushed down on his feet, moving the recliner back to its original position and sitting up. "I assume forced labour built the pyramids of Egypt and the Great Wall of China. I can't support force."

"The migrations that settled the prairies of the US and Canada might work for your tunnel," Sam said.

Brett looked at him. "I like that. We could start with merchandising to capture the imagination, enough daring to challenge the spirit, enough structure to allow development with patches of anarchy, enough front-end commitment to encourage most to persevere to the finish, all leavened with goodwill and spiritual content to ease the soul."

Jeremy said, "Pass the soul food."

Sam glanced over. "What're you talking about?"

Jeremy smiled. "Dad's talk of easing the soul made me think a bottle of beer might help until the Stamps wake up."

Brett stood and paused by his chair. "Now that you guys have brought up the tunnel, I want some help in choosing a name. One restless night, I decided the project should be called Soul Star. What do you think?"

Sam looked at his dad. "I think it's perfect, Father Larson. You should turn your collar halfway around."

Jeremy saluted with his beer bottle. "Sam can tease if he wants, but I think Soul Star's a beautiful name. You done good, Dad."

Sam watched the Stampeders miss a field goal. "Where do a million individuals live for ten years? What do they eat? Who teaches their kids? Who watches out for their safety? What animals migrate through the right-of-way? How is the environment affected? How does one address the issues? How does one manage a project this big? How does one let creativity and imagination thrive?"

Brett turned away from the game. "The answer is chunking, extreme chunking."

Sam glanced at Brett. "I thought a chunk was a poor golf chip."

Brett laughed. "I see chunking as a way to break big challenges into manageable pieces."

Jeremy adopted a theatrical pose. "But once chunked, how do you put Humpty Tunnel together again?"

Brett punched his son's shoulder. "The last resort will be all the king's horses and all the king's men."

Elaine brought down a platter of nachos. "How's the game?"

Sam groaned as he reached for a chip. "The Stamps are getting their butts kicked so we're building a tunnel. We've chosen a name—Soul Star."

Elaine turned to the stairs. "Brett's folly has evolved into a family conspiracy. My dream retirement is morphing into a soulful flight to the North Star."

Brett brought out a batch of sketches showing cross-sections of the tunnel, cross-sections of the roads, pipelines, rail lines, underpasses, bridges, and living quarters. He showed the sketches to his sons. They added ideas, challenges, angles, and risks.

Brett looked up from the sketches. "Do you two remember our trip to the Yukon? We talked about the hardships, the cold and loneliness. You guys enthused about the excitement of the dance hall girls and adventures. Erika dreamed of rich miners competing for her attention. The range of perceptions covered death, drudgery, cold, greed, treachery, excitement, promised riches, and fresh country."

Jeremy said, "I remember the river valleys where gold dredges scarred the channels with mounds of gravel."

Brett handed a cross-section sketch to Jeremy. "The tailings from the tunnel will yield an average surface berm 213 meters wide by 30 meters high, clear across the country."

Sam looked over Jeremy's shoulder. "How do you justify such a scar on the landscape?"

Brett bundled up the sketches. "I pondered that for days. I generated perspectives and justified the surface effects. Nomadic civilizations don't flourish. Societies built on permanent residences tend to mar the natural landscape. The more dense the population, the more intrusive are the structures on the surface."

Jeremy drained his beer. "Seismic lines mar the forested areas for generations. Forestry, power lines, dams, wind farms, roads, and bridges have impacts on the environment. Individuals throughout the world have accepted some level of infrastructure."

Brett put the sketches in his filing cabinet. "The route of the tunnel crosses sparsely populated areas. Few individuals have ventured into the areas near the right of way. Many more will take the route once the road and rail lines are built."

Sam glanced at his dad. "The natural resources will be exploited, though. Clear cutting of trees will generate criticism."

Brett returned to his recliner and said, "These considerations come down to a question of development or no development. We've chosen development."

Sam went back to his chair to watch the end of the game. "I wonder how the world will react."

The Stampeders scored two touchdowns in the second half. The guys climbed the stairs and looked at the girls' Christmas cards. A gold star shone in the top right corner of every card.

Maybe Elaine's protests camouflage some tiny support for my dream.

Chapter 7

Keith Zisemo answered his phone. "Hello."

"Howdy neighbour, how you doing?"

"Hi, Brett, it's been awhile."

"Too long, I'm lousy at keeping in touch. What's new in Mexico?"

"Cheryl and I just returned from a hike along the Cuchumatanes Mountains. We'll stay in Taxco for two months and then snorkel in the Grand Caymans."

"It's a tough life."

"Yeah, I'm enjoying retirement."

"That's the wrong answer. I have an idea."

"I can't hear you. The cell reception is bad."

"You can hear me and you'll be hooked."

"Okay, what's on your mind?"

"Well, I want to build a utility and transportation corridor across Canada from the Pacific to the Atlantic and I want all the vested interests to accept the results."

"So give God a call."

"I've got him on the line."

"Yeah, right."

"I have an idea, will you listen?"

"Sure, but no promises."

"My concept involves a comprehensive set of utility-transportation corridors on a hundred kilometer grid across the entire country."

"Your grid should hit every Indian Reservation in the country."

"I know; that's why I called you."

"What can I do?"

"I want all vested interests on side. I have an approach but I need some expertise."

"Can this magic be described in two sentences?"

"Maybe half a dozen."

"My cell will die after a while."

"I think of an open collaboration on the internet where a map of Canada is set up so that anyone can review the data up to the moment. We'll encourage anyone to record the coordinates of every conceivable spot that should be protected from the corridors and adjacent activity. From that data, the most appropriate corridors will emerge. But we'll still need to address all of the concerns of natives, environmentalists, landowners, and political factions. New issues will be raised as the probable corridors become evident and attention is focused on specific sites."

"It'll have to be easy enough to use so that a casual internet searcher won't give up. Do you have a solution?"

"Yes, I want to design a website that'll allow open collaboration—along the lines of Wikipedia. It'll have to impress anyone who opens it so that we start a stampede to help solve the corridor issues. We need a launch position in which any participant should see the potential."

"Will this website flutter down from the stratosphere?"

"No, you'll build it."

"Good night, Irene. Good night, Irene. I'll see you in my dreams."

"Come on, Keith, you have skills. You're a few months into retirement. You have a chance to do some good. Pay it forward."

"I told Cheryl I'm so thankful that I don't have to tolerate all the crap involved in business. Now, you ask me to dive in again. Do you think I'm insane?"

"The symptoms are there."

"Let me think on it for a bit. I'll call you next week."

"Thanks, Keith. I appreciate it." A thumb up punctuated his gratitude.

Chapter 8

Early morning, the phone rang. "Brett here."

"Good morning, Brett, it's Keith."

"Have you decided to pull your sombrero over your face and forget I ever existed?"

"No; I like the corridor idea. I want to play a part. However, I don't want to give up all the plans that Cheryl and I've made. I'm fed up with Canada; I want to spend most of my time in Mexico."

"Thanks, Keith."

"I know a guy in Calgary who's capable of the day-to-day operations. The guy would need a salary but the Zisemo Foundation will provide an annual grant large enough to support a core office, salary, and computer support."

"Do you need the board's approval for the Foundation support?"

"Yes, but I have made enquiries and I expect the board will approve the project."

"What happens next?"

"I agree to be a mentor to the project. We need to ensure I can stay in the loop from Mexico or wherever our travels take us."

"What can I do to move it along?"

"I suggest you sponsor a weekly coffee party that'll include you and six guests. The guests will rotate out after three sessions. Out of these sessions, you should build a base of ideas. If you video those sessions, you can make the videos available to all current and past guests so each participant can see what evolves and submit further written feedback."

"Yeah," Brett said, "I can make that happen. Anything else?"

"You could find a sketch artist with exposure to highways, railways, bridges, and bullet trains. Invite him to watch the videos and sketch various designs. These sketches will be available to every coffee party participant."

"Okay, what about all the interest groups?"

"I think we should engage researchers to seek out detailed information on the demands of interest groups. Have you made a list of the factions?"

"Yes, First Nations land claims, environmental concerns, political platforms, land owners, and existing laws."

"Okay, we need to figure out how to gather that information."

"What if we issue a challenge to all departments of all universities, colleges, technical schools, and high schools in the world to provide suggestions?"

"That should work. There are opportunities for consideration by engineers, environmentalists, sociologists, psychologists, philosophers, anthropologists, actuaries, and a bunch of others. While the focus of the challenge is the Canadian example, the spin-off of the concept is applicable in every country. The British former colonies have many similarities including British influence, native populations, adherence to the rule of law, and democracy. The rest of the developed world has parallel challenges with variations. There are advantages for the less developed countries where built infrastructure is less dominant."

"We could arrange public recognition for effective design solutions," Brett offered.

"Projects never end unless there are target dates. What timeframes do you see?"

"The public launch of the website might be on Christmas day as a Christmas present to every Canadian. I've thought of a name for the project. The rights-of-way could be called Ribbons and the protected sites could be called Jewels. Do you like the name, Ribbons & Jewels?"

"Yeah, I like it."

"Once Ribbons & Jewels is announced to the public, it will be in the public domain and have a life of its own. I'm excited now; don't tell me to get lost!"

"Keith, you've made my day. Thanks a bunch."

Brett wondered, this appears too easy; is Canada ready for rational approaches to issues that have festered for years?

Chapter 9

Myrtle Murdoch, publisher of the Prairie Sentinel, sat in a coffee shop in Winnipeg. Rosie Savard joined her.

"What credentials do you bring to your position as manager of the Healthy Habitats project?"

"I grew up with my native Indian mother on a trap line in northern Manitoba. At six, I went to live with the Yudzik family in Winnipeg. They helped me get an education. I have an anthropology degree and I'm committed to the environment. I decided I'd make environmental sense out of development initiatives in northern Canada. As I cast about for an opportunity, I ran across the initiatives of the Zisemo Foundation. It seemed like a good fit, so I hired on as the researcher for the First Nations aspects of Ribbons & Jewels. Keith Zisemo noted my enthusiasm. We perceived the project as neither pro nor anti-business and needed to raise more publicity. Keith asked me to help find a sponsor to further the effort. The Foundation agreed the Healthy Habitats Society could best carry Ribbons & Jewels to the public. It fell to me to convince Healthy Habitats to sponsor the project. My experience, passion, and reputation led to my appointment as the manager of Healthy Habitats' Ribbons & Jewels project. This is a wonderful opportunity. I'm determined to succeed."

"I want to do a feature on your story in my paper," Myrtle said. "Is that okay?"

"Yes."

"May I take your picture for the article?"

"Sure, but the picture you need is the photo Jack Yudzik took of my mom when she realized I'd have a chance in the white man's world."

"How do I get that photo?"

"You need to ask two people: Jack Yudzik and Hymie Friedenberg. Both of them have rights to the photo."

Myrtle wrote down the names she mentioned. "We could visit a long time, but I believe I have the substance. If I need more clarification, I'll be in touch. Thanks for your help."

"You're welcome."

Chapter 10

Myrtle sent a copy of the Prairie Sentinel article to Jack and Hymie.

Jack read the article. It carried him back twenty-one years.

He couldn't sleep. The opportunity accorded with his convictions. He encouraged individuals to do the right thing. Cecile could have perceptions on this opportunity that could wreck his family, maybe his life. The easy course would be to forget about Rosie.

Are good and bad things random, part of a plan, or pre-ordained?

He recalled stories where individuals prayed for God's intervention, failed to act on opportunities presented, questioned God, and heard God say, "Three times I came to you and three times you rejected me."

In the damp chill of his autumn camp twenty-one years earlier, Jack had decided to act. He would go to Cecile and ask for her support. He'd also explain to their daughter, Theresa, who would soon be seven years old. Jack packed his gear and headed for the designated lake where the chartered Cessna would take him to Flin Flon, where he would pack his Land Rover and head to Winnipeg.

A wealthy New York hotelier commissioned Jack to photograph a unique image of a caribou. No more instructions than that.

On his first trip into caribou country, he found caribou and studied their habits for six days but found no memorable moment.

155

He told Cecile of his fruitless trip and encounter with Young Eagle and Rosie. Cecile covered the spectrum from amusement, to concern, to anger before she trounced off to bed.

Not the envisioned welcome home.

Two days elapsed with scant thaw in Cecile's demeanour. She explored her feelings toward Jack, the threat of a woman in Jack's targeted territory, and the disruption that a Métis girl would cause in their midst. But she also thought of Jack's kindness, his love of nature and people, his drive to do the right thing, and his love for her. She arranged a sitter for Theresa and prepared Jack's favourite meal. When Jack came home, Cecile greeted him.

"Will you be okay if I try to understand?"

Tears welled in Jack's eyes as he hugged her.

"Come, I've prepared dinner; tell me about Rosie and how we make this work."

Jack explained how their family might provide a home and hope for one little girl. Cecile warmed to the possibilities. She trusted Jack. On selfish and superficial levels, she could bite. Jack picked up Theresa at the babysitter's by eight-thirty. As they walked home, Jack asked Theresa, "Would you appreciate a good friend that could become a sister?"

Theresa looked up at her dad. "I'd like a sister that's blonde, knows about princesses and famous places, and imagines travel to faraway places."

Jack laughed. "What if the little girl didn't know any of that, but she knew lots about surviving in the north, hunting, fishing, and watching the night sky?"

Theresa hesitated. "Maybe, but it seems strange."

Jack and Cecile couldn't afford to hire a plane to search for Rosie. Jack called his New York client and described the situation. Jack's goodness and the opportunity shone through. The New Yorker offered to pay for a charter plane large enough to carry Jack, Cecile, and Theresa to the trap line to search for Young Eagle and Rosie. If Young Eagle and Rosie agreed, they would fly back to Flin Flon and drive to Winnipeg where Young

Eagle could stay for a few days and Rosie would start her new chapter.

The bush pilot said, "You're going to pick up a native girl who's never been off a trap line and take her to live with you in Winnipeg. Are you crazy?"

Cecile raised her voice over the noise of the plane. "That was my first reaction, but we've decided each individual should try to make the world a better place."

Jack had discussed the options with the girl's mother, saying she should move to a small town where the girl could go to school, but the mother concluded that she couldn't be happy off the trap line and couldn't see a way to make a living. Besides, she felt her daughter would fare better if she learned to live in the white world.

"Jack's philosophy is in tune with this project," Cecile continued. "Theresa and I are committed to make it work."

The pilot glanced back at Cecile. "I've been around natives all my adult years. Their culture is so different from the middle class in Winnipeg. I can't see this working out."

Cecile leaned forward in her seat. "Do you check the fuel and instruments before you take off in this plane?"

"Of course."

"Do you know about a snag, frozen in the ice and covered by a skiff of snow? That snag is going to catch the skis when you land and topple this plane, end over end. Our lives will be different than before."

"I know there are risks. I've heard the truism that there are old pilots and there are brave pilots, but there are no old, brave pilots. We're trained to be cautious and alert. I'm confident in my abilities."

"You have a little advantage over us because of pilot school. We go into this as caring individuals who have parented one child for seven years and observed life in Winnipeg for thirty odd years, but we have not gone to school to learn how to integrate a half-breed six year-old into our Winnipeg culture. We plan to be cautious and alert but we will fly."

As they flew into the trap line area, all watched for signs of Young Eagle and Rosie. On the third pass over the area, they spotted a woman, a child, and a sleigh pulled by a dog. The pilot made two low passes over the woman and then landed on the nearest frozen lake. The Twin Otter came to rest near the shore and all scrambled out. The pilot gathered twigs and branches and started a fire. Jack readied his camera and noted the light conditions. The trappers emerged from the trees. They moved with purpose but no hurry to this unknown rendezvous. As Jack came into Young Eagle's focus, her jaw tensed but she made no move to welcome him.

Cecile stepped forward. "You must be Young Eagle and Rose Mary. Jack has told us of your dream, so our family—Jack, Theresa, and I—have come to offer Rosie a home so she may get the opportunities you seek for her."

Jack focused his camera on Young Eagle's face. As the enormity of the offer entered her consciousness, Young Eagle's face lit up in a way that's seldom captured on film.

Young Eagle demonstrated genuine appreciation but she refused to go with the group back to Winnipeg. She asked Jack to write their address on a piece of paper and to describe how to get to their home. Then she walked away from the fire with Rosie and explained what was about to happen. Rosie faced separation from every familiar thing: her mother, her home, her territory, her comfort zone. Six years old, stoic, familiar with risk, heart beating rapidly, Rosie stifled her sobs and stood by the plane. Cecile began to question the wisdom of this endeavour. Theresa grappled with the clothing, smells, and sounds of these apparent family members. Jack wondered whether the right thing is the right thing. The pilot busied himself with the plane.

Chapter 11

Twenty-seven years of age, Rosie stood in the boardroom of the Healthy Habitats Society and presented the outline of a feature series on Canada's environmental fabric that she believed would inspire the readership and provide impetus for effective environmental controls. For every "but," Rosie responded. The board asked her to stay in town for two more days. During that time, they'd do some due diligence and decide if they could commit the Society's resources to this task.

They summoned Rosie to the boardroom.

The evasive faces telegraphed failure.

She turned to leave. "I expected more."

The chairman stood. "Ms. Savard, we want to do your project but we haven't found a way to fund it."

Rosie turned. "Give me your plan and your budget and I'll find the funds." She left.

The chairman gestured with both hands. "Comments?"

One director shifted in his chair. "I like the Ribbons & Jewels idea. I think it's a good project for Healthy Habitats, but I don't see how we can work with that dynamo."

Another director looked up. "Dynamos are in short supply."

The chairman settled back in his chair. "There seems to be enough merit in this situation for us to schedule a special meeting to discuss it further. Can we meet two weeks from today?"

They scheduled the meeting.

Chapter 12

"This meeting is called to order. We consider the potential sponsorship of Ribbons & Jewels as offered to us by Rose Mary Savard. Aaron volunteered to organize information for this meeting. Aaron, go ahead."

"Several capable individuals have developed this project. Keith Zisemo is an accomplished executive who has retired to Mexico but is a mentor for Ribbons & Jewels. Brett Larson owns and manages a prominent development and construction company in southern Alberta. They organized focus groups in which several experienced individuals produced a series of videos that illustrate the magnitude of the issues. They hired a sketch artist who prepared hundreds of sketches inspired by the ideas emerging from the coffee parties. The group decided a reliable database is required to make sense out of the many angles. This database is already developed with masses of data from available sources. The database needs more attention to design the website capabilities before Ribbons & Jewels is announced to the public. The Zisemo Foundation hired Rosie to research the First Nations aspects of Ribbons & Jewels. She's well regarded by all of the individuals that I contacted in the last two weeks. We already know Rosie's capabilities. In my opinion, the Ribbons & Jewels initiative is solid."

"Do you have the videos and sketches?"

"Yes; they're set up and ready to run."

The board watched the videos and sketches and discussed the issues.

The chairman straightened his papers. "I believe the last couple of hours have demonstrated this board is interested in sponsoring Ribbons & Jewels. Am I correct?"

The directors murmured assent.

"I detect general approval. Aaron will inform Rose Mary Savard that the board has authorized her to work with Healthy Habitats' management to develop a plan and budget with mutual expectations that Healthy Habitats and Rose Mary Savard will find adequate funds before significant expenses are incurred."

The chairman called the question. "All in favour?"

"Carried, unanimously."

Chapter 13

Three thousand delegates assembled. Rose Mary Savard waited in the wings. The emcee strode to center stage. The crowd cheered, then stilled.

"Ladies and gentlemen, the moment has arrived: Healthy Habitats presents Rose Mary Savard."

Rosie walked to the podium, smiled, and waited.

When the audience silenced, Rosie began.

"Passionate friends, welcome!

"Today, together, we launch a bold experiment.

"Each one of us comes here with an agenda.

"That agenda has evolved from our backgrounds, cultures, commitments and perceptions about big business, politicians, and tree huggers.

"Our experience has taught us to distrust other factions in our society.

"We're here today to lead a fresh, positive, cooperative process.

"We bring commitments to specific causes but we recognize that others have alternative views, and we will reach compromises.

"We will protect elements of each environmental issue and we will allow for other considerations that are important but less critical.

"We will build a consensus and we'll promise to abide by the spirit of that consensus.

"We must not fail! We will not fail!

Tunnel Vision

"We are familiar with prominent corridors in our great land: the Yellowhead Highway, the Queen Elizabeth Expressway, the CN and CP rail lines, the Confederation Bridge, the St. Lawrence Seaway, the TransCanada Highway, to name a few.

"We know that service corridors are essential in our final plan.

"We expect all submissions will concede that service corridors will exist.

"We choose to call the corridors ribbons, a symbol for the concept of corridors for utilities, vehicles, trains, boats, tourists, and other situations where unfettered human and commercial movement is warranted.

"Development near appropriate service corridors is an economic reality.

"Our challenge is to design a system in which such development coexists with the whole environment, including those issues for which you are passionate.

"Canada will have human habitats.

"We will design models that minimize the negative effects on the environment and protect habitats and unique sites.

"We must not fail! We will not fail!

"Each community has sites that are precious to the local population and, often, to the broader population.

"We think of Niagara Falls, the national parks, the provincial parks, the municipal parks, the Plains of Abraham, the site of the Duck Lake Rebellion, the Medicine Tree, cemeteries and burial grounds, rare animal and plant habitats, the paths of migrating animals and birds, the spawning runs of fishes, and the feeding traits of wild animals, fishes, and birds.

"Each of you endeavours to keep these sites and concerns in focus as well as issues that are of particular importance to you.

"We want you to use your passion but we want you to recognize that the universe involves balancing forces, even when humans are absent.

"You will achieve more for your cause with a degree of collegiality than you will with, 'It's my way, or no way.'

Dave Amonson

"We choose to call all these sites and special issues jewels. You can think of jewels along the lines of Crown Jewels, Marilyn Monroe's diamonds, costume jewels, birthstones, horseshoe nail rings, dandelion necklaces, whatever.

"The jewels have different importance to different individuals.

"The environmental and historical jewels that will be protected will be those that have broad support amongst the human population.

"Most of us will protect unique jewels.

"Your challenge is to put your jewels in a light that will allow them to survive the many compromises that we will face.

"There are infinite perspectives concerning the jewels in Canada.

"We will publicize the identification of the jewels so every discovered issue is taken into account when the plan is published.

"We recognize there are elements of many environmental issues that are not well understood. One of Healthy Habitats' commitments is to continue to encourage the discovery of new issues and promote improvements in habitats, protect unique sites, and future development in concert with current knowledge of environmental issues.

"Each of us recognizes that humans will impact our environment.

"If we adopt a 'stand still' approach until every environmental risk is discovered, researched, and publicized, we know that human initiatives will continue to erupt in unpredictable, confrontational, wasteful episodes with the vocal, best funded, most strategic interests able to carry the day.

"This is not the way to protect the environment, nor is it the way to manage our human endeavours.

"Some of you are guilty of enjoying the game.

"You may start with a legitimate environmental issue but end up addicted to conflict and one-upmanship. Individuals who thrive in this milieu are recruited into various environmental

165

causes. Such gamesmanship must be managed so we get the 'best solutions' with minimal friction.

"With your diligence, permeated with goodwill, many thousands of Canadian jewels will be protected.

"We must not fail! We will not fail!

"Every project benefits from milestones.

"We have prescribed such milestones.

"Initial submissions will be submitted by December 31 this year.

"There are several intermediate milestones to propel the project, but suffice to say a final plan will be published in the December issue of Healthy Habitat magazine a year and a half from now. It will be a Christmas present to every Canadian.

"It will feature a map of Canada, show the identified Ribbons & Jewels, discuss the issues, and promise to publicize jewels with attention to advocacy of 'doing the right thing' for the environment. The printed maps will be supplemented with a digital set of layers that will show the suggested ribbons and the identified jewels. This will permit individuals to identify jewels that will be protected, vulnerable, compromised, and lost if the ribbons remain as chosen.

Where habitats are compromised, the maps will suggest where similar habitats could be developed nearby. This effort might apply to wetlands and forests.

"Canada is a wonderful country.

"We can provide effective environmental protection in concert with human endeavours.

"Canadians, and humans the world over, count on us.

"We must not fail! We will not fail!

"Passionate friends, do it well!

"Thank you."

The activists operated in confrontational systems where they perceived business did the bare minimum and publicity often involved civil disobedience and obstructionism.

How would this new dynamic unfold?

Chapter 14

Gaston Tribolski went for a beer with a teammate after the hockey game.

Josh poured his beer into a glass. "You seem reserved. What's up?"

"My job's frustrating me. I've got to get out of there."

"Is it the job, or is it you?"

"Who knows, my supervisor's ill-suited to his role. He resists innovation, emphasizes cost control over results, and dwells on due process. The place breeds frustration."

"It sounds like you want a project where you can be in charge."

"But I don't have management experience."

"You won't learn to manage by following...especially your supervisor."

"Where'll I find a job that suits me better?"

"I read an article about the Ribbons & Jewels initiative in the north. I'll find the article and bring it to work tomorrow. We can meet for lunch and talk about it."

At lunch the next day, Josh handed Gaston the magazine. "The article describes the extraction of information from every published article in every Canadian newspaper, relevant autobiographies and biographies, published speeches, Hansard transcripts, environmental studies, and court cases...all done by volunteers. The Healthy Habitats Society adopted the cause as a cornerstone of its commitment to healthy habitats."

"I remember something about it. A woman gave a speech about a system of corridors throughout Canada."

"Yes, her speech triggered a deluge of submissions. Healthy Habitats recognizes that the volume and variety of Ribbons & Jewels responses demands more from its data management system."

"Maybe my provincial health ministry experience would be useful."

"The woman is named in the article. Give her a call."

Rosie returned Gaston's call and discussed the issues with him. She liked Gaston's potential. She arranged for the lead IT guy at Healthy Habitats to join her in a meeting with Gaston. The meeting went well. When Rosie determined that Gaston would accept a position with Healthy Habitats, she asked the chairman of the board what step to take next. The chairman arranged for the entire board to meet with Gaston so that each of them could judge his suitability.

Chapter 15

Rosie and Gaston entered the boardroom and accepted coffee. The chairman informed the group that Aaron Woodman, the vice president of the environment, would lead the discussion. After introductions, Aaron directed questions to Gaston.

"How do you see any interested party getting access to the data we've already gathered and the data we will gather?"

Gaston described his ideas in detail.

Aaron asked Gaston to explain how he saw the submissions being integrated into a coherent design.

"It appears to me that some system must be developed where the front end information is neutral and subjected to quality control but any participant can point out errors or improvements. These suggestions must be available to all who wish to review the validity of the front-end information. This will require qualified manpower."

"How do you see the corridors emerging from this mass of data?"

Gaston explained his ideas and answered the questions that arose.

"What do we do with the impossible and the passionate responses?"

"This is where Healthy Habitats will lead. We'll maintain neutrality. We'll request civility. We'll encourage compromise. We'll shift the corridor to reflect consensus. Through much iteration, a democratic solution will emerge. Healthy Habitats must not stop there. We must reach out to the advocates of jewels that are compromised by the corridor. Collegial, compassionate, genuine consideration of the advocates' submissions must shine through. Maybe overpasses or tunnels or some other solution will emerge. The result must be transparent, thorough, and fair."

"I thought you came here as a technical wizard; what's with all this empathy and philosophy?"

"Rosie asked me what would happen if my employer let me out of a locked room in the basement. I told her. She liked it. Here I am."

"I do too. Are there further questions from the board?"

The vice president of humanity asked, "Should we discuss First Nations issues and how to manage those issues?"

Aaron turned to the director. "I considered that line of enquiry and concluded that none of us have enough information to reach a decision. Therefore, I've decided to focus on Ribbons & Jewels. We must develop a strategy to deal with the First Nations issues, but that's a task for another day. I hope the board will accept my approach."

No other questions or comments arose.

The chairman walked around to Gaston. "Mr. Tribolski, we thank you for meeting with us today. I feel certain that the board would ratify your appointment today. However, so much depends on this appointment that I want to ensure that each board member considers your appointment over the next three days. Then we'll meet, debate, and decide. Once we've decided, we'll inform Ms. Savard and ask her to convey our decision to you. Whatever the decision, I want to complement you on your approach to life and this project. Thank you."

Gaston and Rosie thanked the board and left the room.

Out in the hallway, Rosie said, "That was beautiful."

Gaston blushed. "Thank you."

Each wondered what to do next.

They said goodbye and parted.

Chapter 16

Ribbons & Jewels published the viable corridors for major infrastructure from east to west and north to south.

The Ribbon most suited to Soul Star stretched from the St. Lawrence River mouth near Bersimis to the southwest corner of the Yukon. A short stretch of Alaska lay ahead, then the Pacific Ocean.

How do we get access to the Pacific with Alaska in the way?